PRAISE FOR
THE FATHER EFFECT

"John Finch is a man with unstoppable conviction and heart. His new book, THE FATHER EFFECT, is a strong debut worth reading."   —Dr. John Sowers, author of
The Heroic Path and *Fatherless Generation*

"John's story not only deserves to be heard, it offers hope to all men and boys, and should be heard. He stands victoriously upon the stone that once weighed him down and from that foundation shows how we can be free through forgiveness."   —Dudley Hall, president of Kerygma Ventures
and author of *Men in Their Own Skin* and *Grace Works*

"What starts out as a gripping personal story accelerates quickly into a hard-hitting, larger story of today's epidemic of fatherlessness and how that crippling wound snowballs down the generations—until one son determines to face it, disown its shame, and press ahead into genuine manhood."
—Gordon Dalbey, author of *Sons of the Father:*
Healing the Father-Wound in Men Today

"Father wounds don't heal with time. They must be addressed with love and forgiveness. In his book, THE FATHER EFFECT, John Finch addresses the real pain associated with this wound and how it affects our ability to be a father to our children. I highly recommend this book for those wanting to address their own father issues as well as those seeking to be equipped to be a great father!"

—Tom Lane, author of *The Influence of a Father* and
lead executive senior pastor of Gateway Church

"With courageous vulnerability, my friend John Finch paints
an emotionally gripping portrait of the undeniably powerful
impact a father (or lack of one) has on the lives of children.
THE FATHER EFFECT is a story of brokenness, redemption,
and vision for finding healing the only place it can be
found—in the gospel."   —Kris Dolberry, men's ministry
specialist of LifeWay Christian Resources

"THE FATHER EFFECT is desperately needed today...
Because John Finch has been deeply wounded himself, he
knows the powerful healing that Jesus Christ offers through
His wounds that heal us and His resurrection that redeems
us. May those who recognize their own wounds through this
book also find healing from the same Word made flesh Who
healed John."   —Fr. Mitch Pacwa, SJ, PhD

"THE FATHER EFFECT is a revealing, honest, and moving account of one man's experience with the wound created by the
tragic death of his father when the author was eleven years old.
That story will undoubtedly prompt men to reflect on their
own relationships and perhaps wounds from their fathers. It
will also inspire readers by hearing about the role of faith and
the redemptive power of forgiveness for paternal shortcomings. Much wise and useful advice is contained in the book for
men who are searching for ways to become the type of father
they wish they'd had."
—George W. Holden, PhD, Department
of Psychology, Southern Methodist University

THE FATHER EFFECT

THE
FATHER
EFFECT

Hope and Healing from a Dad's Absence

JOHN FINCH
WITH BLAKE ATWOOD

Unless otherwise noted, all chapter opening quotes are directly from *The Father Effect* documentary.

This book is dedicated to the five most amazing and important women in my life:

my wife, Michelle; my daughters, Ellie, Brooke, and Sydney; and my mom, Pattye.

I would not be the man, husband, and father I am today without all of you.

I love you more than you will ever know, and I am one blessed dude because of you.

CONTENTS

CONTENTS

FOREWORD

As a pediatrician who has practiced medicine for a little over thirty years now, I've heard just about everything that a child or adolescent can say about life and their parents. I've listened to the hearts of thousands of children, and much of what I hear troubles me deeply. I've heard girls as young as five years old cry over their missing fathers. I've held hands with sixteen-year-old boys sobbing from anger they feel toward themselves for having "driven away" their dads. Young children and teens who feel the deep hole in their hearts from having no dad wonder if life is actually worth living. Children can't reconcile that they are not responsible for their father's behaviors, because they lack full brain maturation and cognitive skills. They simply can't process the pain that even many adults have difficulty processing.

I have watched the divorce rates rise alongside the concomitant swell of depression, anxiety, increased sexual activity, drinking, drug abuse, ADHD, and learning issues in children and teens. Children who don't have fathers in their homes or engaged in their lives suffer terribly. It's high time that we as a culture do something for our kids—and that is, help their fathers. We must stop demeaning and shaming dads through movies and sitcoms. And we mothers must stop criticizing their every move, because if a father doesn't feel respected in his family, real disaster can ensue. As Emerson Eggerichs writes in *Love & Respect*, every man needs respect in order to live a healthy life and be a good father.

We in America are facing a national crisis. We see teenage boys in inner-city gangs killing one another because they are out of control. Why? They have no fathers. We see teenage girls having sex with boys they don't even like, because they long for male attention and affection because they have no fathers. The crisis of fatherlessness doesn't affect just the inner cities—it spans across America into the homes of middle- and upper-middle-class families who may have a father present but see him disengage. He may not do so willfully, but simply because he really believes that he has very little value in his children's lives. How can he know his value if he is not taught, affirmed, or encouraged?

When fathers "orbit" or leave their homes, something deeply painful happens to the mothers and children who stay. The children feel the ground beneath their feet crumble. Women become angry and resentful. And the men who disengage end up in very dark places.

I am so grateful that John Finch knows this. I am sorry for the pain he endured as a child, but without that life experience, I don't know that he could have produced such a profound work as this very important book. With the keen skill of a surgeon, he peels back the coverings of fathers' lives to expose the tragedy that lies beneath for many of them. He astutely walks men and women through their father wound-edness by helping them look back over their lives and face their grief. John takes us through that process empathetically because he bravely walked through it before his readers. He turned inward first and faced his own father wounds. There-fore, he is the perfect guide for anyone who has lived with a disengaged, absent, or abusive father.

The Father Effect is an extremely important book because John puts his index finger on the pain points in our country, in the hearts of men and in the lives of children who grow up without their fathers. Best of all, he offers hope to all who read, for healing, redirection, forgiveness, and the knowl-edge that they *can* be great parents. They *can* raise great kids and lead a full and wonderful life.

The Father Effect, however, is not just for men. It is a book that *every* woman should read as well because they, too, suffer when they have bad or absent fathers. Women who are hurt by their fathers often grow angry, bitter, depressed, or anx-ious and usually carry that pain into their relationships with their husbands and children. Thus, the vicious cycle of hurt perpetuates itself.

We have a crisis on our hands. I dare say that if we as a nation don't begin to take the impact that fathers have on children seriously, we will see our children face far bigger problems, our families torn apart, and more children killed. When the family loses its father, it weakens and crumbles. And when families deteriorate, neighborhoods do as well. Towns then suffer along with states, and finally our nation weakens. Let us clearly see the breadth and depth of this fatherlessness issue in our country and homes. We are dealing with children's lives and the health of a great nation. Let us be strong enough to resolve to care for men and teach, encourage, and inspire every father we know. If we want to leave a mark in this world, let us be about the business of following the instruction John gives us in this wonderful book.

Meg Meeker, MD

Best-selling author of Strong Fathers, Strong Daughters and the country's leading authority on parenting, teens, and children's health

PROLOGUE
LETTER FROM MY FATHER

April 10, 1979

To My Darling Wife & Sons whom I dearly love,

I couldn't do something illegal & immoral to get money to pay the bills. It would hurt you all so much more and God might not forgive me. I know of no other way to keep from hurting you more. I don't understand why other than from my own weakness that this came to this. I ask for your love forgiveness and pray for God's forgiveness. My last thoughts are of each of you and I pray that each of you Pattye, Larry, Scott, and John will live this life in truth and love and that you will know that I truly loved you with all my heart.

All My Love,
Dad

To My Mother, Wife & Sons, whom
I dearly love,

I couldn't do something illegal or
immoral to get money to pay with.
It would hurt you all so much
more and God might not forgive
me. I knew of no other way to keep
from hurting you more. I don't
understand why, other than from
my own weakness that, I has
come to this. I ask for your
forgiveness and pray for God's forgiveness.
My last thoughts are of each of you
and I pray that each of you Mother,
honey, Scott & John will live this
life in truth & love, and that you
will know that, I truly loved you
with all my heart.

ALL My Love,

Dad

INTRODUCTION
THE DAY I KISSED MY DAD GOOD-BYE

"Hold on, son."

As a forty-year-old man, I wept while holding the picture.

Big Jim is squatting, and I'm sitting in the crook of his right arm. My two older brothers stand by us on each side. They're smiling. I was too young to know what to do.

Big Jim's wearing blue coveralls, and we're in a well-maintained, grassy area. Flowers dot the landscape. A white, nondescript building sits in the far background, but if you look closely enough, you can see bars on the windows.

We're visiting my dad in prison.

But it's not the picture itself that makes me cry. It's knowing what I now know about my dad: how the lack of a father in his life led him to make many bad choices that eventually sent him to prison and ultimately, I believe, drove him to suicide. I felt sorry for the man in the picture whom I'd hardly had the chance to know.

Yet the reason I could empathize with him was that I *was*

him. The final gift my father had left for me was an unyielding burden I shouldered throughout my teen years and well into becoming a father myself.

As I cried over that picture, I could almost hear Big Jim say the phrase that still echoed from my childhood, spoken by the man I once wanted to be: "Be a big boy, John. Be a man."

Decades later, I still wondered: *Am I? Am I a man?*

I asked myself this question for most of my life because no man told me I was doing a good job, or that I was a good husband and a good father—because no one affirmed me as a man.

THE DAY I CAN'T FORGET

"Hold on, son. You owe me a kiss."

I ducked my eleven-year-old head back into his car and kissed my dad good-bye. I walked into school as if it were any other day, though I knew something was different. My dad was seldom in town long enough to take me to school, but my fifth-grade mind thought little of it—aside from feeling lucky to have been dropped off by Big Jim.

That afternoon, we watched a movie in class—another stroke of luck. I felt privileged that I was allowed to sit *on* my desk instead of behind it. In the middle of whatever semi-educational fare we were watching, the assistant principal came to our classroom.

"Finch? John Finch? Someone's in the office to see you."

The day was getting stranger by the minute, but the strangeness had so far paid off well. I was a good student, and

I'd seldom been to the office for anything. I obliged without a word and without fear.

In the office, I saw the last person I would have ever expected: my pastor.

He was curt. "John, we need to go to your home."

I don't think he said anything else until we pulled up to the apartment where my family lived.

As soon as I saw my mother standing on our balcony in the middle of a throng of people I didn't know, I knew something was very, very wrong. My lucky day that had begun with the rare treat of my father chauffeuring me to school was about to take a drastic turn.

Throughout the day, people kept visiting. More arrived. A friend of mine from church came over. We tried to play outside like it was any other day. I'm fairly certain I just kept staring at the cloudy sky above.

I didn't know it that day, but I really had kissed my dad good-bye.

THE QUESTIONS I COULDN'T ANSWER

I lost count decades ago of how often I've replayed that day.

Because answers were so fleeting, hypothetical questions attempted to fill in the gaps: What if I had been a better son? What if my dad had known how much he really meant to me? What if I had told someone about the gun I'd found in his closet two weeks before that strange and terrible day?

He knew I'd found it, too. His brief but stern warning to me—"Don't you ever tell anyone you found this. Now get out of here"—ensured my silence, until now.

Of course, as an eleven-year-old, each of those questions revolved around *me*. I assumed I'd done something to make my dad do what he did. At the time, I didn't know what I know now. I had no idea of the kinds of inner demons he'd been fighting for almost his entire life. Like a child whose parents are divorcing, I blamed myself for what was totally out of my control—because I wanted to, somehow, make sense of such senselessness.

Maybe if I had said "I love you" more often.

Maybe if I had defied him and told my mom about the gun.

Maybe I'd still have my dad.

And maybe my life would have been completely different.

But it wasn't.

I became my father's son.

And I knew that if I didn't change, I was going to lose my family, too.

THE WAY FORWARD IS THE WAY BACK

This book chronicles my thirty-year journey to become the father I was created to be despite my own father's absence from much of my life. It's the story of how I learned to forgive my father and in doing so found a freedom unlike anything I'd ever known before.

The reverberations of my father's seemingly selfish actions echoed within the emptiness I felt for so long, until God led me to a deep understanding of and empathy for the man who was seldom there for me. As a struggling father of three daughters myself, I knew that their futures relied on my coming to grips with my past.

INTRODUCTION

I had to change my life to change my legacy.

This book also serves as a companion to my documentary, *The Father Effect*, a feature film relating my journey to forgiveness. The documentary features some of the smartest Christian minds on fatherlessness, including John Eldredge and Dr. Meg Meeker. I also interviewed dozens of adult children of absent fathers, who shared their stories of seeking to forgive the men who had failed them where it mattered most. Unless otherwise noted, the quotes used within this book are from the film. Some excerpts are straight from the documentary. Others are from material left on the cutting-room floor, which simply couldn't fit into the documentary but is no less insightful and revealing.

When I began filming, I naively believed that my work was mainly for the benefit of others like me: grown adults trying to live normal lives despite a persistent, long-lasting, gaping father wound. But what I learned from those teachers and heard in those stories resulted in nothing short of a deeply transformative work in *my* life.

I am a full-time husband, father, and businessman who knows the panic of seeing glimpses of his absent father within his own soul. But I also know the hard-won joy of forgiving my father, even when he'll never return.

To forgive my father, I'd have to be exactly what he'd always asked of me: a big boy—a man.

To forgive the man who'd taken so much from me, I'd have to confront him.

Even worse, I'd have to empathize with him.

PART I
TO FORGIVE MY FATHER

CHAPTER 1

WHO WAS BIG JIM?

"I think every person has this longing to know what their father was like when he was little."

For years I denied how deeply my father's death had affected me—and not just me, but *all* of my relationships. I didn't want to get to know the man who had inflicted such a deep wound on me. To forgive my father, I knew I'd have to learn more about him.

There was so much I didn't know, and not just about *that day*.

What was he like as a child? What were his parents like? How long did his dad stick around? Was he happy as a kid? What were his friends like? What did he do when he wanted to goof off? What did he excel at? How did he meet my mom? These questions spawned more questions.

Everything within me screamed in righteous anger over being asked to discover my father's history. I felt like a child who's burned his hand on the stove being asked to forgive it.

If he hadn't cared about me, then why should I care about him now?

Internally kicking and screaming like the adult-child I was, I began to learn about my dad.

What I discovered changed my life.

MY FATHERLESS FATHER

When Big Jim was nine-year-old Little Jim, his father died of pneumonia. In other words, for most of his life, my dad didn't have a dad.

Though Big Jim would never have called it by name or likely even acknowledged its existence, my father had a deep father wound of his own. This alone broke my heart for him, but it was the progressively complicating factors of his life that would cause me to deeply empathize with this man I'd known for only a short while and with whom I'd been angry for decades.

Two years after his father's death, Big Jim's mother married a man who she later found out was *already married*. To escape embarrassment, they moved from Millington, Tennessee, to New Orleans, but moved back just a year later. Before marrying my grandfather, Van, she'd been married four times. I surmise that my dad's emotional and relational growth as a man was severely stunted because of his upbringing. He'd lost his dad, only to have multiple fill-in fathers let him down even further.

My dad also had to deal with a mean mom whose dual mottoes were "Only the strongest survive" and "Every man for himself." Consequently, he sought to become the strongest man for himself with as little help as possible from anyone else. In looking over the many bad decisions he'd go on to make during his life, it would seem that these intrinsic values seldom served him well—especially when it came to being a father.

At sixteen, Big Jim was dropped off in New Orleans to live on his own. To make enough money for lunch, he'd hunt for scrap metal before school started. Six years later, at just twenty-two years old, he married my mom. As further damning evidence of the kind of parental support my father rarely, if ever, received, his own mother didn't even attend their wedding; nor did she care to, from the stories I've heard.

Big Jim and my mother had known each other for years before getting married, as my dad had been inseparable friends with her brother, Bill. Big Jim and Bill both excelled at football, so much so that my dad was once offered a tryout with the Green Bay Packers. For reasons unknown, he never tried out.

It's stories like these—the ones where a single choice may have led to a drastically different life for both him and me—that give me pause. What if he had tried out? What if he had made it? What if money hadn't been such a big problem for him? What if he had been rewarded for what he excelled at?

The fatherless are unrivaled at the what-if game.

Even from this brief biographical sketch, it's easy to see that so much of what I was missing from Big Jim was the same as what he had missed from his own dad. His father had died when he was a child. Later in life, he became an entrepreneur (of sorts), always out for that one big score that would solve all his problems and secure a future where he would never have to worry about money. He thought he had to be the strongest or the best to gain respect and provide for his family.

And I don't have proof of this, but I assume it's true because it's been true for me: He was desperately lonely, believing he was the only one enduring the struggle known as life.

When I finally chose to stop defining my dad by his worst qualities and tragic end, I discovered a man with a father wound just as deep as mine.

He may have been my father, but we were brothers.

HOW TO BREAK INTO FORT KNOX

At one point in his life, my dad owned four tire stores appropriately named "Big Jim's Tires." A natural salesman, he did well for a time. The stores made money. Our lights stayed on.

But my father was susceptible to the promise of easy money. Through his business, he met men in organized crime who ran a counterfeiting operation. There's likely no easier way to make money than just to print your own.

Unless you get caught.

My father got caught after stepping off a plane. He was promptly sentenced to the Federal Correctional Institution in Texarkana, Texas, for two to five years. But just eight months later he was released for good behavior. His conscience—or his desire to stay out of prison—had spoken up. To commute his sentence, he had agreed to turn state's evidence *against* the men with whom he'd been counterfeiting money.

Now, recall that these men were in *organized crime*. Think

The Godfather. These were not men to be trifled with or to turn on. Yet my father, in what I hope was a turn toward doing the right thing (and not just to save himself), willingly chose to testify against these coldhearted criminals.

While still in prison, he would travel from time to time to testify for the prosecution against these men. And with each piece of damning testimony from my father that put away more men, you could be sure that others in their criminal organization were taking note.

A few months after my father was released from prison, the FBI called to inform him that his name was the last on a hit list, below the names of three people who had recently been killed in violent ways. His name was next to be crossed out, and they suggested that he and our family go into witness protection to avoid danger. We were to relocate to Fort Knox, of all places. I can imagine my dad's response: "You're gonna put a known counterfeiter *in* Fort Knox?" A few days later, we started packing.

As an older child, I had faint memories of being taken from my home in the middle of the night, but I'd argue with myself that it was only a dream. However, when I became an adult and learned the truth—that the FBI really had absconded with my family in the middle of the night when I was just two years old—I couldn't argue against reality anymore. We really had lived under witness protection in Fort Knox, as "the Smiths" no less.

We lived there for ten months. Ironically enough, the men who'd put out a contract on my father's life eventually became state's witnesses themselves, effectively canceling the contract. The FBI cleared our family from any imminent threat, and we moved to Texas.

Did my dad leave Fort Knox with a gold bar or two? I don't think so, but memory's a funny thing. Knowing what I now know about my dad, I wouldn't have put it past him.

HOW TO STAY OUT OF PRISON

My dad couldn't quit his fast-money lifestyle, even though our lives had all been put in jeopardy because of his inability to work for a living on the right side of the law. Big Jim's checks bounced like overinflated basketballs. Our electricity was cut off multiple times. Mom even had to heat our water so we could have lukewarm baths. Bills wouldn't be paid for months at a time.

Sometimes we stayed in hotels where calling the accommodations "squalid" was being nice. In fact, I recall my mom placing an ironing board against the front door as a rudimentary burglar alarm. If it fell, we'd all hear it, wake up, and shout in fear. Then, I guess, my mom would have thrown the iron at the intruder. Thankfully, no such event ever happened.

My dad ran away from his problems, but he would always try to find a quick fix, regardless of its legality. He would disappear for a few days, only to return with a sly smile and a proud declaration that he'd solved our problems yet again. Much to my mom's chagrin, he'd act as if nothing had happened. Yet it was my mom who was truly the savior and would somehow scramble to get the money to pay the debts my dad had left behind.

I assume that my dad tried the best he could to provide for our family. Unfortunately, he'd had no example growing

8

up of how to do that. How can a man understand what's required of a father and husband when he doesn't have anyone to show him or tell him how to be a provider?

There's no telling exactly what he'd done to get the money we'd needed, and I doubt my mom asked him for fear of incriminating herself. But, as had happened before, Big Jim's poor choices caught up with him.

On April 10, 1979, my father's lawyer told him he was most assuredly headed back to prison after his court meeting later that day. Before that date, my father had reiterated to my mother dozens of times that he would *never* go back to prison. And though I didn't know it at the time, he'd also read medical books to figure out the best place to shoot yourself so you'd die the fastest.

He held to his promise. He never went back to jail.

On April 10, 1979, my dad shot himself.

CHAPTER 2

ANGRY AND ABANDONED

"Because my dad chose to abandon me, I was very bitter, angry, and resentful, and it was impacting every aspect of my life."

I always assumed my friends, classmates, and everyone else in town thought, *That's the kid whose dad killed himself.*

Although I was usually the biggest kid in my class, I was also likely the most insecure. After all, I didn't know anyone else whose dad had committed suicide. I walked to my classrooms with a self-defining scarlet letter emblazoned on my heart. Even if no one else could see it, I knew it was there. Although I lived with two older brothers and a strong mother who unconditionally loved and cared for her children, I was easily intimidated by others because I hadn't learned how to act like a man. My siblings did their best to fill the gap, but they were still just my brothers. During some of my most formative years, I didn't have a godly male role model to give me direction, guidance, and wisdom about the world, about girls, and about what a man should say and how he should act.

Once my older brothers moved out of the house to attend college, I spent even more time learning how well my mother loved other people. But this had a dual-edged effect on my personality. Instead of growing into boldness, strength, and courage, I grew into kindheartedness, tenderness, and care. In other words, I took on the characteristics that were most often displayed in my home. I just thought I was "the sensitive type." It wasn't until much later that I learned I was sensitive because I didn't know any other way to be.

Despite my mother's deep affection and care for her sons, she would never be able to overcome the deficit that had hollowed out our lives when our father had chosen to take his life. To make matters worse, I couldn't talk to Mom about how I felt. I didn't want to add to my mother's burden. I never wanted to disappoint her. But, as yet another example of how an absent father leads to so many seemingly never-ending cycles, I obviously couldn't talk to my dad about my problems either. He couldn't tell me that I was doing a good job at school, or that everything was going to be okay, or even that he'd beat up that other kid's dad for calling me names. He couldn't help me process my failures. He couldn't do anything. He was gone.

One issue that frustrated me the most was not having a father who would help me learn how to persevere in a world that can often be so hard on its residents. When the going got rough, I quit. In high school, I quit football. Even now, I regret that decision and still dream of having another chance to make a better choice. Even though that was my decision to make, I still blamed my dad for not being there to tell me,

11

"Hang in there, son. Life isn't easy, but if you quit everything, you'll never succeed at anything."

This led to the creation of a lonely person who was fearful, distrustful, and afraid of what the future held. So I kept my head down, focused on my studies, and tried to make sense of my interior world that was never meant to support itself without a fatherly foundation.

ACCOLADES AND NEW ADDICTIONS

As questions about girls, school, sports, and every other issue important to a high schooler kept arising, I became increasingly bitter and angry that I couldn't talk to my dad about such things. My mom—bless her—attempted to fill in the gap, but our conversations were generally brief. I knew she was trying but that she really couldn't help me. And I certainly wasn't going to initiate the conversation.

So I took the route that most aimless, fatherless young men take: to try to look cool in front of my friends.

For me, that meant drinking, partying, and sleeping around in college, aka: what I thought real men did. Because I didn't have a father figure invested in my life, no one had ever told me or shown me what a real man does. I thought access to the "real man's club" was through the doors of booze and babes. So I began drinking in high school, a terrible addiction that would enslave me for the next two decades. I didn't know it at the time, but I drank to numb my pain. As an added benefit, being the life of the party awarded me with the attention and affection I'd been craving my entire life.

I became addicted to it.

On the outside I was having a blast.

But I was a ticking time bomb within.

ANGER OVER WHAT WAS

Following my father's suicide, I became an angry young man, which is so normal that it's become a stereotype. As one of the five stages of grief, anger is to be expected with the passing of any parent, but my anger wasn't seasonal. It didn't last for just a month or a year or a decade. Until God changed my life, anger dominated me, but I was rather good at disguising it.

I was angry with my dad for willfully choosing to leave not just my family, but me personally.

What right does he have to choose for me not to have a dad for the rest of my life? How selfish can he be? How can a loving dad do something so spiteful? Doesn't he understand how much I need him and will need him for the rest of my days?

For so many decades, I couldn't understand his frame of mind: how he couldn't think beyond his immediate present to see anything worth living for, like his wife, like his kids—like me.

That anger increased whenever I thought about praying, especially in the days and months after my dad's death. I blamed God. If He was so good, then why did He let that happen? If He was so powerful, why didn't He make the gun not work? Or why didn't He force me to tell my mom about the gun that day I'd found it?

If I prayed in those days, my prayers were angry questions cast into a seemingly uncaring sky.

Though the anger would seep through in more stressful moments, I was adept at masking the pain—until I had kids. It's not that my kids made me angry—at least no angrier than any parents' kids might make them—but I was constantly mad at myself. I was disappointed by my severe lack of fathering skills. With a vision of who an ideal dad was, I always felt that I never measured up, and this frustrated me to no end. I was forever disillusioned by my own expectations of what a father should be. And that would start the cycle of angry blame all over again: *Ultimately, this is your fault, Dad, for not being there when I needed you and not being here now when I need you. And it's Your fault, too, God. Thanks for nothing.*

I'd get angry when I couldn't do something simple in the house because I didn't know how. Feeling inept would raise my anger and reinforce feelings of abandonment and worthlessness. I believed that I never lived up to my wife's or my children's expectations. I was never good enough, and I blamed this feeling on never receiving such confirmation from my father.

Early on, before I knew about the father wound and how much it had affected me, I didn't know that so much of my anger stemmed from my past. But even when I knew about the cause and effect in my life, I still wouldn't open up about it. I'd either drink it away, party it off, or isolate myself so that I'd have no one but myself to get angry with.

That's not a healthy way to live. And it's certainly no way to grow as a man.

Although most people wouldn't have described me as an angry guy, I was a kettle constantly near its boiling point. If any event raised my stress levels by even one degree, I'd bubble over, and my anger would burn any who had the misfortune to be near.

In those early days, I often thought of my dad as a coward who had taken the easy way out while leaving behind a wife and three boys. Soon after my dad died, I vowed that I would never, ever be like him.

But as I grew into what I thought was a man, I mimicked his life for far too long, becoming more and more like my dad with every passing year. I desperately sought what I desperately needed, but I was often too drunk, blind, and angry to see what I really needed: to forgive him.

CHAPTER 3

THE POSER AND THE ADDICT

"Because I did not have a dad walking alongside me giving me guidance and direction, I was desperately looking for any and all signs that told me I had what it takes to be a man."

As a fatherless child who grew up in Section 8 housing, who always searched for attention, who was hypnotized by the world's definition of success, and who drank to numb his pain, I was a prime target for living it up as best and as long as I could on the company's dime. I was a salesman who traveled the country and had been given what seemed like carte blanche decision-making power (coupled with a ridiculous expense account) to wine and dine any prospective clients. My life was a paradise.

Except paradise to an alcoholic is just a slowly drowning hell. I was a crab in boiling water too numb to realize his inevitable outcome.

I spent more money than I ever could have imagined on alcohol at bars and restaurants, on golf at some of the best courses in the country, and on tickets for sporting events. I was living the high life and taking no prisoners. I'd finally "made it" and had all that I believed I needed to show the world I was a success.

Finally, I was a man.

Looking back, I know that I was trying to prove to my long-dead dad that I could be successful on my own. I wanted to prove—to a world that didn't know it needed proof and to a dad who'd been dead for many years—that I was man enough to go it alone.

My "success" came at a much higher cost than just my corporate write-offs. When I'd arrive home from these weeklong, business-sponsored benders, I'd be hung over, a worthless mess of a husband and father who was useless to his wife and daughters when they needed him the most. After being both mother and father to our three girls for a week, my wife desperately needed to tag out, yet she couldn't allow her impaired husband to take control of the house.

Ironically enough, I wanted to do just that. I'd try to reim-plement my shallow authority with new rules mostly fash-ioned around *my* needs—quiet and sleep—on those week-ends at home. But my ever-patient wife would remind me, "You don't get to do that. You haven't been here all week. You don't know the rules. Just go back to sleep."

Though it hurt me to hurt her, I didn't know any other way through the pain. I'd go back to sleep, get up the follow-ing Monday, fly to God-knows-where, drink God-knows-what, and repeat the same vicious, empty, depressive, hurtful cycle the next week.

Like so many thousands of men before me, I thought

I could find momentary peace at the bottom of an empty bottle. But it was oh-so-fleeting, and the moment after brief contentment washed over me, I'd feel desperately empty within and not have a single clue as to why I felt that way, despite the mounting evidence that my wife was almost through with me, my daughters didn't know me, and maybe "success" wasn't what being a man was really about.

As I'd later learn, drinking wasn't my actual problem. Drinking was the salve I used to cover up my father wound. And even when I began to understand that I had a father wound, I was in full denial about its power. For four long years, I lived a luxurious-looking life, but I was slowly losing all that really made it worth living. I wish I could say that I had a moment of clarity, or that I peered into my daughters' eyes and fully realized how much my life was adversely affecting theirs. But I was too selfish then. I couldn't see beyond the labels I'd worn so proudly for so long.

I wore those names without remorse because I thought they described what I feared I wasn't: a real man. As a young man in college and a single guy in my early twenties who was partying, drinking, and sleeping around, I was proving to the world (and myself) that I had what it took to be a real man. And in my twisted way of thinking, the drunker and wilder I got, the bigger man I was. Ironically, as a married man with three daughters, I once nonchalantly spent $5,000 of company money for the sake of two clients at a gentleman's club, and I truly believed I was the world's biggest man. This was how distorted my view of what a "real man" was.

Because I'd come from nothing, I really wanted to be

something. I thought that throwing money around, drinking with the boys, and ogling women defined what it meant to be an American male. Yet everything I did was subconsciously motivated by my deep-seated, insatiable desire for affection and affirmation.

I drank to numb the pain of what I'd lost. I acted wild to be seen as the cool, fun guy others would always want to be around. I pursued professional success at the expense of my family to feel the all-too-momentary warmth of hearing, "Job well done, Finch."

After years of this kind of living, God revealed a brutal truth to me about the way I'd been living. Buried beneath the labels I'd stacked upon my chest for decades was the one label that truly named me: poser.

JOHN WAYNE FINCH

When shame, self-isolation, and denial team up and attack a man's soul, they're effective at cutting him off from friends, family, and God. They work in tandem and in secret to keep a man's deepest hurts from ever being revealed and consequently from ever being healed.

It's as if men stay like small children who, out of fear of the doctor's office, never want to see the doctor, even if their appendix is about to burst. They just don't understand that health lies on the opposite side of revealing and healing the hurt.

I include myself in that cohort. I didn't want to admit my wound for so long because I was ashamed of it. *Why should this still be an issue for me? How could my dad's death really be re-*

lated to so much else in my life? He left like thirty years ago! I mostly know what I'm doing, and I learned a long time ago to do it without his involvement. I'll be fine.

Famous last words, especially for an alcoholic.

I denied my hurt because the culture told me, "Man up. Admit nothing. Be John Wayne." But my adult mind knew better: John Wayne was an actor. Even if he got shot, he didn't experience pain. It was all fake. That's why he never had to admit weakness.

I tried to be a man as best I knew how, which wound up looking like the cheapest TV rendition of a stereotypical traveling, partying, boozing businessman. I was searching for anything and anyone who would affirm me as a man. It just so happened that this endless search allowed me to simultaneously run from my real issue: dealing with my father's death.

In time, I realized a transformative truth: Pain is a fact of life. Until we admit to having been scarred by its arrows, we will continue to live in denial and not be the persons God created us to be. No real healing could begin until I was able to admit to being deeply hurt by my father. But I was so blinded and comforted by the warm amber haze of my drinking problem that I just couldn't see a way out.

I PROMISE—*I PROMISE*—THIS IS THE LAST TIME

I barely slept the night before because I knew I was going to have the paid-for opportunity to get drunk the next day.

I was particularly excited about this trip to Nashville because I knew my client was a lot like me. Actually, all I really knew was that he liked to drink like me and he was probably an alcoholic. But since neither of us would cop to such an admission of guilt, we took solace in the culturally and corporately acceptable rationale that "this is just how business is done." The fact that my company was paying for our debauchery didn't hurt.

Even though we met only once a quarter, this client and I already had a routine. Anxious to get to what we both desired, we wouldn't even meet at his office. I'd head straight from the airport to the Nashville strip, where he'd meet me around four in the afternoon in front of our bar of choice for that night. We'd imbibe cheap drinks until 4 a.m., just hours before my early-morning flight back home.

On one of those occasions, as I drove myself to the airport while still legally drunk, I made the drunkard's plea with God:

God, I know that I could get a DUI right now. I'm sorry. I'm so, so sorry. I know I've done this a thousand times before, but I promise—*I promise*—this is the last time. The last time, God. Really. I promise this time. I'm never going to drink again. Promise. Just don't let me get caught. And let me get home okay. And don't let my wife be angry. Then I'll quit drinking. I promise.

I paused. Guilt and shame bore down on me like the jumbo jets flying overhead. Knowing that I'd just lied to God for the thousandth time about a devastating sin issue that had debilitated me for decades, I told God something I'd never prayed before. I spoke the words out loud: "Lord,

You are going to have to slap me upside the head to get my attention."

Just a word of advice here: Never challenge God. It won't end well for you.

Four months later, at a golf course of all places, I got slapped.

CHAPTER 4

THE FATHER WOUND

"You just don't get through this world without a wound."

You grew up without a dad, right?"

I picked up my golf ball and stared at my friend Keith. "Yes."

Before he could reply, I went on a ten-minute offensive: "But my mom was and is the most incredible woman on the planet. She's the best mom I could have ever hoped for. She took care of me and my two brothers for years after my dad decided to leave us and the world. She worked herself to the bone to provide for us. We might have been poor, but she treated us like kings. And despite everything she'd endured, and just her day-in, day-out single-mom existence raising three rambunctious boys, she always looked for ways to help other people. She was so loving, too. She loved my father, and when it was just her and her boys, she tried her absolute best to be two parents in one. She was phenomenal."

My friend paused for a second and then asked me, "But was she a dad?"

I might have dropped my golf ball. "No. No, she wasn't a dad. You're right."

Tears formed at the edges of my eyes as I realized the full weight of what my caring friend was trying to get me to understand. His five-word question had neatly summarized so much of what I felt was off about my life.

She wasn't a dad.

He allowed me the time and space in that brief moment on the golf course to feel the depth of our discussion. Then he spoke words that would alter the course of my life: "You have a father wound, John. It's deep and it's painful, and if you don't deal with it now, it's going to impact the rest of your life."

WHAT IS A FATHER WOUND?

I'd never heard of a father wound before, so I searched for anything I could find on the topic. Gordon Dalbey's *Healing the Masculine Soul* was an early and insightful read. I read it in 2007, and I was shocked to learn that it had been written fifteen years earlier, as if this "father wound" thing was a recent discovery. In time, his book led me to similar books by John Eldredge. I devoured them. They reiterated what I'd felt for so long but didn't know how to name.

Essentially, the father wound is something a father has said or done (or hasn't said or done) that has left a lasting, negative effect on a child. The wound can be inflicted in a shocking variety of ways: A dad can hit a child. A dad can curse a child with his words. A dad can set impossible-to-achieve expectations. A dad can work too much and justify his time away because he's financially supporting the household. A dad can be home all the time but emotionally checked out, more interested in checking e-mail than in being intentionally present with his wife and children. A dad can even be physically and emotionally present, yet never say the words every child needs to and longs to hear from their dad: "I love you," "I'm proud of you," and "I believe in you." A dad can never affirm his child by choosing to remain silent in a critical moment when that child needs to hear his or her dad say something—anything. And a dad can choose to shirk the responsibilities of this world by deciding to take himself out of it.

The father wound shows no bias to male or female, or to age, race, or religion. No matter who you are, what you do for a living, or how much money you make, if your father hurt you by effectively abandoning his duties as your dad, you've suffered a father wound.

The breadth of the father wound may be matched only by how deeply it cuts into its sufferers. Some of the world's highest achievers have lived—yet still thrived—with gaping father wounds. One could argue that their respective wounds forced them to seek affirmation in other areas that ultimately led to worldly success.

President Barack Obama can recall spending only one month with his father, back when the former president was only ten years old. He shared about his own void in growing up with an absent father in a 2007 Father's Day interview: "As somebody who grew up without a father in the home, I have a pretty good sense of what that means, and the long-term void that isn't filled when a father's not in the home."[1]

Dennis Rodman is a five-time NBA champion considered by many to be the best rebounding forward in NBA history. Through tears during his 2011 NBA Hall of Fame acceptance speech, Rodman spoke about his absent father: "I never had a father. My father left me when I was five years old. He has forty-seven kids in the Philippines. I'm the oldest one. He wrote a book about me in Chicago, and he made a lot of money, but he never came and said hello to me."[2]

Despite being a billionaire and the cofounder of Apple, Steve Jobs suffered the painful effects of abandonment. Walter Isaacson, his biographer, who spent many hours with him before his death in 2011, shared Jobs's story through the eyes of a colleague and friend: "'I think his desire for complete control of whatever he makes derives directly from his personality and the fact that he was abandoned at birth,' said one longtime colleague.... Greg Calhoun, who became close to Jobs right after college, saw another effect. 'Steve talked to me a lot about being abandoned and the pain that caused,' he said.... Later in life, when he was the same age his biological father had been when he abandoned him, Jobs would father and abandon a child of his own."[3]

Steve became an example of the generational curse, another devastating effect of fatherlessness that we'll soon discuss.

But back when I first learned about the father wound and how long I'd lived without even knowing I'd been terribly hurt, I felt a strange combination of anger and, well, freedom.

HURT YET HOPEFUL

The idea of a father wound made sense to me. As I began to understand how pervasive the effect of my father's absence had been on my life, it was as if a surgeon were slowly but precisely guiding a scalpel into a wound I'd just learned to live with. It dawned on me that an untreated father wound had shaped my entire life. It had subconsciously distorted my reality, which helped to explain why my friend's five-word question, "But was she a dad?" cast a sudden bright light on a hidden area of my heart that had been affecting my entire existence in subtle yet ultimately devastating ways.

Strangely enough, when I learned about the father wound, I was filled with a sense of *hope*—like the relief you might feel following a doctor's appointment. When I start to ache or something just feels off with my body, I get a nagging feeling: *I should probably get that checked out.* But work and life and fear of the unknown prevent me from scheduling that appointment. Eventually, I begin to worry more about possible problems, so I finally head to the doctor's office. After a thorough examination, the doc provides a diagnosis.

Even if the diagnosis turns out to be bad, there's some part of me that feels hopeful once the unknowns become known. Now that I know what I'm dealing with, I can handle it. Now that it has a name, I can call it out. Now that I know the disease, I'm infinitely more equipped to seek its cure.

I drove away from the golf course on that fateful day feeling an incredible sense of relief. I realized I wasn't weird or abnormal because of everything I'd been struggling with for most of my life. The nameless, unidentified, seemingly incurable disease that afflicted me had a name.

And if it had a name, I assumed it had a cure.

Unfortunately, the cure for a father wound isn't just a Band-Aid. The cure would demand that I reach into the deepest recesses of my most painful memories and choose to forgive the man responsible for that pain. Like most people, I didn't want to go through the pain to get the help I desperately needed.

I wanted a resurrection without a crucifixion.

Facing my father wound was the toughest thing I'd ever have to do—but I'd absolutely do it again.

THE PERFECT STORM

After that momentous day on the golf course, I knew I needed to change, but I was content to stay the same. I thought, *Isn't this just a midlife crisis? Don't most men without dads go through something like this? Aren't we supposed to just buck up, shut up, and go on with our lives? Could his absence really have left such a deep scar?*

After all, I was having too much fun running from my problems. I didn't want to face the monster in the mirror I'd become. I didn't want to deal with all the guilt, shame, unworthiness, insecurity, and fear that constantly simmered just beneath the surface of my "perfect" life. I didn't want to own up to the awful mistakes I'd made as a man, a husband, and a father. I allowed bitterness, anger, and resentfulness to fester within my heart, rationalizing my indecision to take responsibility for my life by blaming it all on a man who'd been dead for more than thirty years.

Maybe it was Satan convincing me I'd be better off not

reaching into the past. Maybe it was pure denial that I'd been so affected by my father's absence. Maybe I was too afraid to admit my weaknesses, too scared to fully face my father (even just the memory of him), and too frightened of what lay ahead if I ventured back into my distant history.

Maybe I still wasn't a man.

Maybe I'd never really know what it truly meant to be a man.

But God has strange and powerful ways of growing boys into men.

THE DAY GOD SLAPPED ME

On February 20, 2009, my life changed. A day of reckoning was upon me, and the old life as I once knew it—the old John I'd so long wanted to flee but could never get away from—was about to end.

In the years leading up to that momentous day, I knew that my world was slowly coming apart at the seams. I knew that the longer I kept playing charades with my life, the more likely it was that someone would find me out. The kid who'd always wanted to be loved and affirmed desperately fought against being known in any real way. When I wasn't amassing labels, I was putting on masks. When I wasn't putting on masks, I was drinking to mask my pain.

I was a social alcoholic. I was such an absent father that I might as well have been dead to my family. Even when I was home, I wasn't home. At forty-one, my metabolism had slowed, my waist had expanded, and my heart had begun to let me know that maybe some of my dietary choices were terrible. I feared losing my job.

I sat in my office with my head in my hands, brooding over every one of these worries. They formed like dark clouds in my mind, all coalescing and congealing into a massive thundercloud. As the cloud loomed larger and lightning began to strike in the distance, I saw myself running for cover—except I was on an open plain with no cover in sight, and the faster I ran, the faster the cloud approached. Suddenly, the roar of thunder was pounding in my ears and I was drowning in the rain.

Back in my study, I was weeping.

I was scared and fully convinced that I was all alone, that no one would ever understand the issues I suffered from—then God slapped me with a memory of a golf-course conversation from just a few years ago.

But was she a dad?

That's all God needed to speak into my life for me to finally and completely surrender to whatever He had planned for me, regardless of the time, embarrassment, or suffering I might have to endure. In some ways, it was my garden of Gethsemane moment, my Damascus road conversion. I knew I couldn't keep going down the road I was on, even for another second.

In a flash, I saw how much of a failure I'd been at trying to do life on my own terms without relying on anyone else—and especially God. I understood that I drank to drown my father wound. I was weary of the rut I'd drunk myself into, and I desperately wanted the only affirmation any man really needs.

Through the tears, I finally told God, "I'm all in."

Even though I'd been baptized as a nine-year-old alongside my best friend (a pastor's kid, no less), February 20,

2009, was my true moment of salvation. For the first time in my life, I had truly and totally surrendered my will and my wants to God. That was the day He made me realize just how deeply I needed Him.

At that moment, my life and my desires changed. God removed my desire for alcohol and replaced it with a desire to drink in His Word and search for the cure to my father wound. That search would cause me to become the last thing I thought I'd ever be: a filmmaker.

CHAPTER 5

THE FATHER EFFECT

"The children of the fatherless all share the same central story."

I've given you a story. Now go tell it."

God impressed those words on my heart in early 2011. I understood the first half but was baffled by the second. God certainly had given me a story—by that point I'd finally forgiven my father—but I knew nothing about sharing my story with a wide audience.

Since learning about the father wound, I couldn't help talking about it with other men. I wanted to know just how pervasive this disease was. Once I got past their rather flimsy defenses and rationalizations, many of the men I spoke to confessed to having been deeply hurt in some way by their fathers. I'd heard that whether it was caused by physical abandonment or emotional detachment, fatherlessness was an epidemic, but it wasn't until I began openly talking about it with a large number of men that I realized the truth behind the statistics. When I began to speak at churches and share more of my story on social media, I witnessed that fatherlessness was just as big of an issue with women, too.

And because I knew how much the father wound had affected my life and family, I empathized with these men and women and the struggles they'd faced and continued to endure. Through those conversations, I came to believe that if I could spread the word about this epidemic, God would take my feeble offering and multiply it like loaves of bread to the hungry masses starving for affection.

Part of me wanted to believe that when God told me to "go tell it," He was just reiterating what I'd already been doing. But I knew that wasn't the whole truth. I wasn't supposed to just share my experiences with others in person.

I was supposed to make a movie about them.

Even though I was (finally) receptive to God's leading in my life, I still wondered what He thought He was doing: *Don't You know I'm just a knucklehead? What do I know about filmmaking?*

To which God replied, *Well, David was just a shepherd. I can do a lot with a little.*

I read John MacArthur's *Twelve Ordinary Men* around this time, which reveals why Jesus chose ordinary, imperfect guys like fishermen and tax collectors to be His twelve disciples. I realized that Jesus had used twelve knuckleheads to change the world. While I didn't expect that kind of reach, God used that book to open my eyes: He *could* use a guy like me, a guy who was willing to share his story of redemption and healing so that others could likewise experience the same kind of freedom.

I just had to tell my story.

HOW TO MAKE A DOCUMENTARY FILMMAKER

Prior to this call on my life, I had zero experience in film production—unless you count watching Disney movies with my daughters. I didn't know a cut from a wipe. So I did what most people on a budget do these days in order to learn a new skill: I typed Y-O-U-T-U-B-E into my search bar. In those early days, I was constantly logging on to YouTube to learn how to shoot and edit film. I went to the Apple Store on a weekly basis to be trained in how to use the filmmaking techniques and effects I'd seen on TV. And I might have watched those Disney movies a bit more closely to see how good stories were told.

Once I decided to become a filmmaker, I shared what God had told me with a few important people in my life. They encouraged me to learn what I could about making a film. Essentially, shooting quality video comes down to two things: lighting and audio. I purchased what I thought was a pretty good camera and started asking friends and social media connections to let me interview them.

Still, I had no idea how the film would ultimately come together. I was excited about learning these new skills but secretly doubtful that I'd be able to pull it off. I feared that the idea could turn into yet another personal project I'd fail to finish. But I can now point to many moments along the way that provided the motivation I needed to keep going.

At the top of that list is my wife. When God first laid the idea for *The Father Effect* documentary on my mind, one of my first thoughts was, *There's no way my wife will go for this. I was essentially an absent husband and father for years, and now I'm going to ask for time off after work and on the weekends to shoot a film?*

34

She'd be crazy to agree, and I wouldn't blame her. I wasn't exactly looking forward to that first discussion about the film.

When I told her what I believed God was leading me to do, she didn't laugh once—though maybe a small chuckle involuntarily escaped her mouth when she heard that I was going to become a filmmaker. She already knew about the journey of forgiveness I'd experienced. After all, she was my first and best witness to the radical change God had brought about in my life. Even though she might have been nervous about what my new filmmaking "career" could mean for my availability at home, she agreed to keep walking down this path with me. Months later she'd tell me that she knew God was "driving this bus," because there was absolutely no way I would have undertaken making a documentary given my complete lack of skills and preparation.

I took that as a compliment.

More recently, she perfectly encapsulated this moment in our lives: "You weren't a filmmaker who'd found a good story to tell. You had a story you knew had to be told and learned how to be a filmmaker."

HOW *THE FATHER EFFECT* AFFECTED ME

The bus officially started moving when filming began in May 2011. Looking back, I have no idea—apart from God's blessing—how I was able to gather so many ordinary yet extraordinary people to take part. I was blessed with the opportunity to speak with and film people of wildly different backgrounds, from the ages of twenty-one to eighty-four, who all either tragically shared the common ancestry of fatherlessness or were experts on the subject. They included:

- a former NFL quarterback,
- two best-selling authors,
- a UFC champion,
- a professional rugby player from South Africa,
- a rabbi,
- a former exotic dancer,
- a university psychology professor,
- a self-made millionaire,
- four prison inmates,
- several counselors and pastors,
- and many "average" citizens who had come to terms with their need to forgive their fathers.

I am indebted to my interview subjects for their time, availability, and brutal honesty. That they were willing to go in front of a camera and discuss their deepest pain is a testament to their characters and proof that God can heal the father wound.

What I once thought was simply a means to an end—to create a film because God told me to—turned out to be the next step of my journey toward becoming the husband and father He desired me to be.

Because I wasn't a filmmaker, I didn't know what rules to break or follow. I was just a guy with a camera trying to tell a story. But I believe that helped me more than it hurt me, spiritually speaking. The more interviews I did, the more God taught me things I could take back and implement in my own home to change my legacy and help me become a better dad. In every story and through everyone I interviewed, God showed me at least one thing I could do differently or better. The more incredible interviews I had, the more I was motivated and excited to know that God was involved and these stories had to be heard.

But after the film was made, I struggled with strong doubts. I argued, *I've told my story. Now do something with it, God!* Yet no doors were opening, and it took a lot longer than I ever imagined to make something happen, with several missteps and detours along the way. I wrestled with God and wondered how the documentary would get released to the world. Wasn't I being faithful to His call on my life and my story?

It was then that a friend shared a great analogy with me about my frustration. To paraphrase, he said, "It's like when you're a little kid who's angry and whose dad has his hand out, stiff-arming your head. You're just swinging away trying to hit him, but you can't, because he's just too big and his arm is too long for you to make contact."

My friend was right. In hindsight, I'll add this: The dad knows his child is angry and lets him swing away until the child gets the anger out of his system and wears himself out. Why does the father do this? Because he loves his child and knows what's best for him. Then the dad picks up his child and hugs and kisses him. This is a father. This is God. This was God and me during postproduction and predistribution. This was my time in the wilderness, and God was teaching me to be patient and to trust Him.

He was molding me into the man He needed me to become for this moment. In fact, I sometimes wonder if this journey was more about my growth as a Christian, a man, a son, a husband, and a father than about anything else. (Of course, I'm still grateful that God can accomplish multiple goals with our meager offerings.)

In interviewing those men and women, I learned that I had an incredible amount of room still left for improvement as a man, a husband, and a father. Every interview was like walking into a seminar about becoming a better father. With every word these men and women spoke, I was receiving an invaluable education in what it truly meant to be a dad. As I shared some of these stories with my brother soon after filming them and how they were making me question how awesome of a father I thought I was, he summarized what was happening in my heart and soul: "John, you're changing your legacy as a father."

He was right, and when I understood that this journey wasn't just about my life but about my daughters' lives, and their children's lives, and their children's children's lives, my motivation to complete the documentary skyrocketed. I wasn't doing this just for me or for the fatherless men and women I hoped the film would reach. I was doing it for my family and the generations that would follow.

CHAPTER 6

MAN'S GREATEST ENEMY

"[That] everyone's going to do to me what Dad did to me is the deep fear."

What do you think your dad was thinking at this moment?"

Rock, the actor we'd hired to portray my dad for the documentary, was trying to get into character. My blank stare did nothing to hide the fact that I'd never considered his question before.

What is a man really thinking the moment before he shoots himself?

How much depression, torment, despair, and hopelessness do you have to be drowning in for suicide to become your only viable option?

When does ending your own life seem appealing?

Had he thought about this before? Obviously, he had. He knew enough to saw off the shotgun so he could reach the trigger. And he'd placed blankets all over the borrowed car so he wouldn't leave as much of a mess.

But if he'd had that much foresight, why couldn't he have thought just a bit further, about how his death would hurt my mom and my brothers? And me?

Big Jim, what were you thinking right before you killed yourself?

"John? John? You still with me?"

"Sorry, Rock. I, uh, checked out there, didn't I? I've never really thought about the question you just asked."

"I'm sorry. I didn't mean to—"

"I know. You're just wanting to get into character."

"But I shouldn't have been so insensitive. This isn't just a character. It's your dad."

I gave a dry laugh. "It doesn't help that you look just like him, and that you chose a blue denim shirt for the shoot."

"I had two options this morning. This one seemed right for the time period."

"Well, not only that; that's pretty much what he wore all the time. Or at least what I remember seeing him in all the time."

"I had no idea."

We looked at each other's shoes in an awkward pause.

"Rock, thank you for doing this for me. I know this is challenging for both of us, but I'm certain it will be used to help thousands of men and women heal their father wounds. For the time being, in answer to your question, let's just assume he was thinking one thing: 'I just want this pain to stop.'"

Rock nodded, closed the door to the car, and stared into the distance past the windshield.

The crew set up the shot, then I watched in high-definition as my father prepared to shoot himself.

EMPATHIZING WITH MY DAD'S DEPRESSION

After we filmed that scene for *The Father Effect*, I excused myself and sat in my truck. The tears I'd fought against in front of the actor broke through my weak defenses. I wept for my dad. I tried to envision what his last day on earth must have been like. I tried to understand why he believed death was a better choice than life. Compassion and emotion overwhelmed me. In attempting to inhabit my father's last day, I realized he must have been fighting man's greatest enemy for a long, long time: the debilitating loneliness of depression.

I empathized so deeply because I once again saw how much like my father I had become. I understood his depression because I'd lived it, too—maybe not to the same degree that he experienced it, as that's something I'll never be able to know, but to such a degree that it certainly negatively affected my life for years.

For the longest time, I didn't have a name for it. Early on in my marriage, I'd call it a rut. Whenever I told my ever-patient wife, "I just feel like I'm in a rut," she'd let me sleep it off. For me, sleep was the remedy to my depression. Sleep was how I'd convince myself that I could get through that rut. I'd sleep for a few hours and awake refreshed and (mostly) fine.

But as I aged, the ruts became deeper, more frequent, and longer lasting. Where the ruts previously lasted only a few hours to maybe a day, they became debilitating to the point where they stole days, weeks, and sometimes even months from my life. Sleeping didn't work. Drinking sometimes did. For the most part, I thought, *This is just how life goes.* I didn't know how to make it stop.

41

I was one of the walking dead as I pretended to care about my real life. My only concern in those moments was my family. I didn't want to hurt them in any way, but I also knew that my depression was taking their husband and father away from them. This was especially true with my girls, who were all young children as I struggled to awaken from my zombielike trances. I was missing out on times in their lives I'd never get back. As I slept, drank, or overworked, my wife valiantly picked up my slack, which only seemed to increase over time.

Trying to free yourself from depression is like building a ladder out of toothpicks when you're stuck at the bottom of a hundred-mile-deep hole. No matter what you do, the hopelessness of your situation only worsens. I couldn't will or hope my way out of my depression. When well-meaning men (who often didn't know my full story) would tell me to "Man up," "Just get over it," or "Snap out of it, you wuss!" I'd nod and laugh, knowing full well it wasn't that easy. In addition to feeling that they had no idea what they were talking about, I'd also think, *Denying depression just makes it worse, like refusing to believe you're drowning when you're ten feet underwater and you know you can't swim.* Still, I'd usually tell myself exactly what any other guy would have told me: "Man up, John!" It wasn't until the last few years that I've shared about my depression with my family and a few close friends.

When the bleakness of depression threatened to overwhelm me, my thoughts would still turn toward my kids. I'd fear that my problems would be passed on to them the same way my father's problems seemed to have been passed on to me. I didn't want to see that happen, and in those moments a glimmer of a better future for me and my family shone through.

But only for a moment.

On the days when hopelessness prevailed, I understood my dad's decision just a little more. Even though I'd once believed that his decision had been only selfish and cowardly because of the devastation he'd caused in the lives of those he left behind, I realized that so much more had been going on under the surface of his strong veneer.

In his day, "mental health" referred only to people in psych wards. It had yet to become a topic of general cultural discussion as it is today. And for a man to admit to being depressed or sad about his life in the fifties and sixties? He would have had to turn in his man card. But now we know so much more about mental health and depression. While a stigma still attaches itself to those words, it's nowhere near the severity or the shame of what they once held. That leads to more questions I ask myself: *If my dad could have told someone else about what he felt, or if he'd known how much the state of his mind affected his life, or if someone could have diagnosed him with depression, would he still have killed himself?*

I'd think about what it would be like to take my own life— but I also knew I could never do that because I was aware of how devastating that would be to everyone I'd leave behind. I was depressed but not suicidal. Yet I also wondered how much longer I could put up with the depression. Maybe my father had endured it for so long that his willpower finally gave out.

I wish I could ask him.

THE DEEP FEAR

Growing up without a dad made me fearful because my father was supposed to have protected me and made me feel secure. For all of my teen years and long into adulthood, I was scared of being hurt because I always felt unprotected. Without the early confidence a father instills in a son that all will be well in the world—even when it's not—I peeked around every corner and prejudged every stranger in my life.

In *The Father Effect,* John Eldredge says, "Knowing that your dad is there for you and that he will never leave you and never forsake you establishes confidence in a boy's heart that he's able to move to a man's world. If that gets wounded, he is going to fear rejection and abandonment for the rest of his life... 'Everyone's going to do to me what Dad did to me' is the deep fear."

This is the foundation of a fatherless child's every fear: *They are going to hurt me just like my father did.* If this resonates with you, I imagine that if you peeled the mask off your every fear, you would discover that this is the chief fear. You simply do not want to be hurt again, and certainly not to such a severe degree, because once was enough.

What's tragic is that such a father wound doesn't necessarily have to be caused by abandonment, death, or divorce. Dr. John Sowers says that even "a lack of words, a lack of affirmation, can be a curse. When a dad's not there, what he's actually saying to you, that you hear loud and clear even if he never says it, is, 'You're not worth it to me to be here.'" That's an unbearable burden for any child, yet it's one that such children carry well into adulthood. And so many of our decisions are then ultimately chosen as a result of one simple, deep, painful question: *Will this hurt me like I was hurt before?*

And because that hurt was so painful, we do the only thing we can to ensure we never feel it again. We eliminate the possibility of getting hurt by removing ourselves from contact with others.

HOW ABANDONMENT LEADS TO SELF-ISOLATION

The depression that accompanies the fatherless like a lifelong imaginary friend stems from the father wound. When a father abandons you, you come to believe that no one else really wants you around either.

The fatherless have significant and long-lasting issues with transparency. We fear that the reason our fathers hurt us, left us, or never knew us was because we weren't worthy to be known. Consequently, we live our lives believing that lie and working as hard as possible to cover up that little kid our fathers didn't want to get to know. After all, if he didn't want us, why would anyone else? So we hide.

John Eldredge puts it even more bluntly and broadly: "Guys, primarily, are faking it—scared to death to be known. We are just terrified that if you really see me, you're going to laugh. You're going to leave. You're going to be appalled."

To fill that emptiness, we work harder so that people might applaud our efforts. We make more money so we might be able to escape our feelings through gadgets and vacations. We seek to increase the notability of our names to earn respect. In countless ways, we look for what we never had. And because many of us never had a father tell us who we were and who we could be, we search in vain for a lifetime trying to figure out, "Who am I, really?"

When I asked Stephanie, a former exotic dancer, about her thoughts on how her dad influenced her view of men, she revealed the unspoken assumption every fatherless child has: "They're going to leave me...They don't care about me enough to stay around." Because she believed the lie caused by her father's absence, his ghost haunted all of her future romantic prospects.

To prevent further pain, the fatherless isolate themselves, and doing so is often contradictory. We could be the life of the party, or the most flirtatious of people, but we wear such an outgoing mask to hide our true selves. We can be alone in a crowded room and severely depressed while wearing a smile.

During the three decades following my father's death, when I was either drunk, partying, or running up exorbitant tabs at my company's expense, I was doing exactly what Pastor Dudley Hall said men like me do: I searched in vain for affirmation that could never and would never arrive from an earthly source. Without knowing my full story, Pastor Hall named nearly every one of my transgressions: "You can find [affirmation] in your wildness—drinking, gambling, whatever. You can find it in your ambition—'I've conquered all this.' You can find it in your sexual prowess. You can find it in competition and athletics. Or you think you can. You can look for it there. Actually, you can't find it."

Such affirmation-seeking isn't a guys-only club either. In *The Father Effect* documentary, Michelle shared, "I was promiscuous at an early age. Drank at an early age. Always searching for affirmation, needing affirmation, not understanding that you are good enough, because when your father—especially when a father abandons you—you feel unloved. I just don't understand how you can know that you have a child in this world and you have nothing to do with [her]." Shannen likewise sought affirmation elsewhere: "I've been married four times...I was looking so hard for security, for somebody to love me and not leave me...I used sex to get love."

The lasting effects of fatherlessness are devastating for either gender, but maybe, as the father of three daughters, I think it's even more catastrophic when fathers leave their daughters. While a later chapter is specifically devoted to the fatherless fathers of daughters, it must be related here that men and women process their abandonment in different ways.

For the most part, and this is just from my personal experience over the course of filming *The Father Effect*, men seem to overcompensate for their emotional shortcomings through vices common to society's idea of men: greed, lust, gluttony, and the like. Women seem to look for their lost affirmation in the arms of any man who shows interest. Either way, the deficit created by an absent father negatively affects his child for the rest of her or his life—and not just in a slight manner.

John Eldredge spoke at length on how the abandonment of a father leads to the loneliness and self-isolation of a child and the adult that child becomes:

> In very severe cases you get emotional attachment disorders. They can't commit to a relationship. They can't experience love—like deep withdrawal, deep hiding. In less severe cases, you'll just get guys who are fairly checked out: don't want to commit to a relationship,

don't really want to invest in friendships with men. You go, "Why do men isolate? What's with the isolation thing?" Most guys don't have friends. When they do get in social settings, it stays pretty surface-level. They're afraid of exposure. They're afraid of rejection... So if it's criticism, then he's hypersensitive to criticism. He can't take just a simple instruction from his boss... Well, that's the father wound. If it was an abandonment, then he's going to fear abandonment. If it's betrayal, as in many divorce scenarios, the wound is a betrayal wound in the man. He's going to fear betrayal in friendships. He's going to fear betrayal from his wife, and so he's going to insulate himself emotionally.

In hearing John's words, I counted my blessings even among the scars I'd inflicted upon myself. With as much as I'd been through and the problems I had caused for myself, I'd at least been able to experience love through my wife and children. Even though that love was a shadow of what it should have been in terms of my family receiving love from me, they showered me with love through my darkest times. Even though I'd checked out of our home for years and had willfully chosen to isolate myself from true living, they remained steadfast. My wife didn't allow me to hide or withdraw.

Before, I had chosen to isolate myself for a number of reasons: I didn't want to talk about my past because the story seemed so big and out of the ordinary. I didn't want the people I'd meet in my life to think what I thought all of my classmates had: *That's John, the guy whose dad killed himself.* I didn't want to saddle people with my issues. I didn't want to reveal that this successful salesman wasn't successful at any-thing else in his life.

But mostly—and I didn't know this at the time—I didn't want to open up my father wound because then it would re-veal the place where I could be most hurt again. Betray me once, shame on you. Betray me twice—well, I'll make sure that never happens. If I don't give you my trust by revealing who I really am, then you can't betray me.

Life stays as is, the rut continues, and John remains alone, filling his time by picking up toothpicks.

To escape my hundred-mile-deep hole of depression, I had to stop blaming my father for abandoning me there. I had to ask God to show me the one person I'd been hiding from my entire life.

I had to ask God for a mirror.

CHAPTER 7

THE GENERATIONAL CURSE OF FATHERLESSNESS

"The greatest legacy you can leave your kids is forgiving your father."

After God opened my eyes to reveal to me the man I'd become, I was shocked to see my father's face as the reflection. In the thirty years I'd spent trying to distance myself from the pain he'd inflicted upon me, I had become him.

I was an absent father. I lived as if only the strongest survive. I believed a real man needed help from no one but himself. I was sure to lose my family. While suicide wasn't an option for me, phoning in the rest of my life certainly was.

I was the man who had for decades told himself, *I'll never be like my dad*, only to find himself walking in his bootprints. Even at forty-one, Little John still emulated Big Jim.

I couldn't help but wonder why that was the case. Why do men with dead, depressed, or disinterested fathers tend to trod their same pathways into adulthood? Why do we become what we detest?

That was one of my driving questions in *The Father Effect* documentary.

"I HAD GOT USED TO IT"

I didn't know Jose's exact age when I interviewed him, but he couldn't have been more than thirty. Then again, maybe prison time adds years to your life like being on TV adds weight.

Jose recalled how his lean ten-year-old body could hardly drag his dad out of a bar, an event that happened more than once. Growing up, Jose also had a front-row seat to the nightly terror of seeing his alcoholic father physically abuse his mother. Around the time Jose turned sixteen and thought he needed to be a man, he modeled exactly what he thought a man was: Jose verbally and physically abused his mother as well.

I was shocked. His experience was so hard for me to comprehend, and yet I had an inkling of what lay just beneath that misplaced anger.

As we spoke, I didn't hear so much sorrow as regret. Jose knew he'd messed up his life, and he also understood the origin of those early, grievous errors: "We could relate that to my father, as far as him allowing me to do things I'd already done and witnessed. I began to think that it was all right to be the way that I was—you know: violent, or rude, or disrespectful to my mother."

In the emptiness of a strong, masculine role model, Jose

modeled the man who was closest to him, even though that man was an alcoholic abuser. Seemingly, he couldn't help but become what he likely hated. As he told me in our interview, "I had got used to it."

BROKEN FATHERS RAISING BROKEN SONS

With the release of *Wild at Heart*, John Eldredge popularized the notion of the father wound to a generation who'd likely never heard of it. He made men feel like it was finally okay to admit to being hurt by the one man they thought would never hurt them. Eldredge's insights in that book, his future books, and throughout his ministry have likely helped millions of people deal with the mess that fatherlessness leaves in its wake.

In *The Father Effect*, Eldredge talks about the father wound's lasting devastation:

> If you want to understand the power of the father wound and how pervasive this is, start with the symptoms.
>
> Men are having a hard time being men. First off, you have all the addictions: the pornography, the gambling, the alcohol, the cocaine, the food. Massive mess. But then you also have all of the brokenness: the rise in suicides among men, depression, anxiety disorders. Then you just have that army of great guys out there who feel like they're blowing it. They don't feel good as dads. They don't feel like they know what to do with a marriage. They don't know how to handle a career. Take all

of this debris. What do you do with this evidence? How else do you explain that?

It all points back to one issue: that deep, profound woundedness in the heart of men and how they mishandle it. Because men are famous for mishandling our own brokenness. It's a source of shame, so we hide it. It's a source of pain, so we go medicate it with something. We do everything but go get it healed. So the result is something profoundly tragic in masculinity in the world.

I can tell you what the crisis is. I can tell you what the cause of that is. You need to heal the heart of men. Then you'll get a man who knows how to love a woman. Then you'll get a man who knows how to be a dad.

I also interviewed Dr. John Sowers, author of *Fatherless Generation*. John has seen, heard, and experienced what the epidemic of fatherlessness causes. While we were at his office in Portland, recent events in his city spawned memories of a trip he'd made to Los Angeles:

Just a little over a month ago, there was a boy shot about fifteen feet from behind where you're sitting, on our front porch. It was a gang-related shooting.

In LA alone...there's ninety thousand registered gang members and some six thousand homicides over a five-year period. You look at that and you begin to go, "Okay, this is a big deal, and who are these kids, and what's their story, and what's driving them?" And by and large, these kids, you'll hear them say they're looking for belonging, for family that they've never had.

When I asked the LA police chief, "Who are these kids?" he said, "They're fatherless. They're kids who are looking for dads." Fatherlessness is the engine driving our most urgent social problems, from gangs, youth violence, teenage pregnancy, drug abuse, self-injury, cutting, depression, high school dropouts, suicide...

If you look at who these kids are, there's one common denominator. It's not lack of education. It's not even social or economic status. It's fatherlessness.

There is no substitution for an engaged and involved father in a child's life. Few doubt that. Unfortunate statistics bear out that truth as well. According to the National Commission on Children, children of absent fathers are:

- five times more likely to commit suicide,
- six times more likely to be in a state-operated institution,
- seven times more likely to become a teenage mother,
- seven times more likely to drop out of school,
- eleven times more likely to commit rape,
- fifteen times more likely to have behavioral disorders,
- fifteen times more likely to end up in prison while a teenager,
- and twenty-four times more likely to run away.

A boy needs a father to guide him into manhood. He needs a father who models how he should act within the world. He needs a knowledgeable father to show him how to fish and hunt, how to throw and catch a ball, how to treat women, how to tell right from wrong, and to show what perseverance, discipline, and sacrifice look like. A boy needs a protective father to save him from himself and others. A

54

boy needs a heroic father to look up to. And a son needs a beaming father who knows when to say, "Today, son, you've become a man, and I'm proud of the man you've become."

Likewise, without a loving father in the home, a daughter will seek the next-best imitation, which may be far from the "best" of men. That's why a girl needs a father to model what it means to be a man who loves, cherishes, and respects women. She needs a dad to show her how the opposite sex ought to treat her. She needs a father who will teach her right from wrong. She needs a dad to protect her and make her feel secure. She needs a father who displays affection, to both her and her mother, so that images of healthy affection outweigh what she sees in the culture.

Children need a verbal father who lavishes encouragement, praise, and love upon them. They need a wise father who lifts them up when they've fallen and helps them interpret failure so they're less likely to fail again. Children need a guiding father who can point them in the right direction, especially when that child is trying to figure out his or her place in the world. A child needs a loving father to provide the singular validation only a father can give his son or daughter. Without such a father in their lives, children stand to experience the same hurts their absent fathers did.

Eldredge spoke to how this cycle of woundedness leads to dads who don't know how to be dads: "Your dad was wounded, your granddad was wounded...you've got broken men raising broken men. You've got broken fathers, and they end up raising broken sons."

And so the generational curse curses another generation.

LIKE FATHER, LIKE SON

The idea of a generational curse originated with God. In Exodus 20:5–6, while delivering the third commandment against making and worshipping idols, God says, "I, the LORD your God, am a jealous God, punishing the children for the sin of the parents to the third and fourth generation of those who hate me, but showing love to a thousand generations of those who love me and keep my commandments."

Eldredge clarifies what such generational curses look like today:

> This is a spiritual principle given to us in Scripture: the sins of the fathers being passed down from generation to generation. You'll find in one family line it's divorce, and you'll look back and go, "Wow, great-grandfathers and great-uncles, and then fathers and cousins—what's with divorce in this family line?" In another family line, it's not that at all. It's alcohol, and it seems like, "My great-uncle was an alcoholic, and then my cousin was, and now I am." Sometimes it's sexual issues. Even things like failure or rejection.

Much like my ignorance about my father wound, I was shocked at how eye-opening and ultimately freeing the notion of a generational curse was to my personal journey in forgiving my dad. I felt like I'd discovered a secret key that would unlock everything about why I was the way I was. Learning about the existence of a generational curse seemed to be the last puzzle piece to the incomplete picture of my life.

This curse was "something that got passed down through a family line, and therefore you can actually get out from under it. It's not just you." When John Eldredge spoke that short last line while we were filming, I felt hope. The truth, as it has a habit of being, was so true.

I thought, *It's not just me. I'm messed up, but at least it hasn't been all my own doing. I know a lot of my suffering was a result of my own dumb choices, but my behavior was a result of my wound and the anger I felt as a result. But it wasn't just me. I wasn't all alone and the only one going through it. There are millions suffering and struggling from the same kind of generational curse.*

Then, when I heard Eldredge speak to the breadth of the curse—that it could include issues like fear and rejection—my heart leaped. He was speaking to me without knowing it.

The generational curse of fatherlessness, where the sins of the fathers *become* the sins of the sons, has been with us for a long, long time. I've heard it said that a father can impact hundreds of generations following him, and I firmly believe that—which is all the more reason why we must discover a way to break the curse of fatherlessness so that the blessings of a father can ring out for *thousands* of generations.

THE CURSE OF FATHERLESSNESS TODAY

Pastor and author Tom Lane puts this generational curse into a modern context within my film: "If your grandad was abusive, probably your dad was abusive. If your dad was abusive, there's probably abusive tendencies in you toward your kids. When you abuse your kids, they're gonna abuse their kids. Why? Because the iniquities—a tendency toward a given area—follows multiple generations."

I believe addictions are passed down from one generation to the next through more than just genetics. While a person may be genetically prewired to succumb to a particular addiction, there's another and more readily apparent reason for their addiction: That's what was modeled for them.

The addictive, aberrant, or abusive behavior children see modeled in their fathers becomes normalized. Without knowledge of what's best, or even what's acceptable, children of abusive, absent, or addicted fathers have no way to know what normal behavior is. Consequently, if their father comes home drunk every night and occasionally punches their mother, the child may feel that something's not quite right, but without the context of what *is* right, the child likely won't understand that such behavior is *far* from right. She or he thinks, *That's just my daddy, and that's just the way things are.*

Men without strong father figures tend to take the edges off their abandonment pain by normalizing their childhoods. Tom Lane shared that when he begins a pastoral counseling session with a new person, he'll simply say, "Tell me a little about your story." Then he hears a devastating story that's made all the more shocking by the storyteller's assent that it was "just a normal childhood."

> They start out saying, "Well, I grew up in a normal family. My dad abused me. My folks were divorced. My dad was in jail for, you know, offenses. Just a pretty normal life."
>
> I realized most men don't know what normal is from a biblical perspective... We think, "Well, my deal isn't any

worse than your deal. This is normal."…And that's the way we operate as men. Until there's a standard that is raised that says, "Wait, wait, wait! What you experienced isn't normal. It's not according to a biblical pattern that God designed, and I can show you a different way." Until we do that…everything's good—and it's really not.

Children of the fatherless are especially adept identity architects.

We must break this deplorable generational curse and begin to live as God has called us to live, as people who refuse to allow poor past examples of fatherhood to dictate our present responsibilities as parents. But before planting our feet firmly in the present, we must deal with what happened to us in the past.

THE HIDDEN CURSE OF THE CURSE

A generational curse is insidious in a number of ways, but its most devious aspect is its ability to coerce you into believing you're simply a victim of circumstance. Living with a victim mentality reveals itself in thoughts such as:

I can't help my drinking problem because my daddy drank.

I can't trust anyone.

Life is just harder for me than it is for other people.

At its core is a feeling of powerlessness and the repeated mantra, "It's not my fault."

For people who have suffered father wounds, this may be one of the easiest—and deadliest—emotional traps to fall into. We tend to believe, "I _____ because my dad

59

_____." Fill in your particular generational curse or your chief self-identifying characteristic. Mine would read "I drank because my dad drank"; and "I was the life of the party because my dad left us."

While there are certainly facets of truth to these statements, people living with victim mentalities believe such statements cover the gamut of their choices in life. In some ways, it frees them to do whatever they want and then blame it on dear old Dad. But in many ways, such a self-limiting belief imprisons them in the past with no power in their present. Like a stuck record needle, the album of their life just keeps spinning and scratching over the same faulty groove. If they have children, they will likely pass on the generational curse despite their best efforts.

To veer away from a victim mentality, acknowledge the hurt your father may have inflicted on you. Weep over it if you must. Talk to your spouse, a close friend, a counselor, or a pastor. Mourn the relationship you could have had. Consider how your father's actions (or inaction) may have resulted in your present-day actions and choices. But don't be so naive as to believe that your father's actions wholly dictate what you do and who you are today.

Don't be a victim; be the man or woman God has called you to be.

As one who's chosen to no longer be a victim and to do the hard work of father forgiveness, I beg you to choose to break your generational curse—for yourself, your spouse, your children, and your children's children. The epically long benefits of choosing to engage in such difficult soul-level work are worth the effort.

But where should you start?

TO BREAK THE CURSE

The further back you pry, the wider your eyes may open to the generational curse of fatherlessness.

Do you know your father's history? Have you heard any stories about his father, or his father's father? How much do you really know about your dad as a child, teenager, or young adult? How much have you heard about his parents, or their parents?

For instance, I was shocked when I learned that my grandfather died when my dad was only nine. But that simple fact helped me come to grips with his actions as my dad. He didn't have a guide to lead him through life or a hero to emulate, so he did the best he could.

As a father decades later, I realized I was the same. In a strange way, God used my dad's fatherlessness to help me have compassion for him. In seeing how God was turning this curse into a blessing, I was reminded of Joseph's words to his family in Genesis 50:20: "You intended to harm me, but God intended it for good." While Satan may have intended to hurt me through the generational curse of fatherlessness, God eventually used it for good.

I was cursed with a father who was cursed as well. That's why it's a generational problem. The sins we fight against regenerate with each new generation. But this understanding—that I had more in common with my dad than I once thought—birthed an inkling of compassion within me. To a degree, I am the way I am because my father was the way he was. For good or ill, I modeled what was modeled for me. What I endured with him may very well be what he endured with his father, and what his father endured with his father, and, well, you get the picture.

Sometimes the poison taints every branch of the family tree.

To stem the tide of that poison trickling any further, you need to replace it with something more life-giving.

Believe that you are a beloved child of God. Know that He is proud of you, believes in you, and loves you more than you could ever comprehend. Remind yourself as many times as it takes that God is your Father, not your father. Nothing you do or don't do will make God love you any less, ever. Regardless of your mistakes past, present, and future, He loves you.

He loves you.

He loves you.

If a full realization of God's love sits at the core of your identity, you won't need to fill any emptiness.

You'll be overflowing.

Here's the thing we often miss when talking about generational curses: Once that curse has been broken—once *you've* decided to pursue father forgiveness so that the cycle ends with you—God promises something even greater: to keep His steadfast love to the thousandth generation.

On my journey toward forgiving my dad, I realized how much God was *for* me, and not just for me, but for my family and my future generations as well. Again, Eldredge pinpointed my turnaround:

> The power of Christianity and the power of the cross to break those things is just phenomenal. You can come out from under that whole legacy of sexual sin...of debt, or failure, or rejection, or betrayal, or whatever it is that's been dogging your heels for years, to experience a greater freedom.

This is also a phenomenal gift you give to your kids. When you draw the line in the sand and you say, "That generational stuff does not pass me. That ends here," what a gift you are giving to your children, your grandchildren, their children.

To stop the legacy here? You're a hero.

Years from now, I pray that my daughters will say of me what pastor and former NFL quarterback Neal Jeffrey says of his father in my documentary: "My dad was not perfect. He had issues. He struggled with stuff all of his life. He didn't have a good influence in his life. But essentially *my dad broke that chain*...and now, praise God, I'm raising my kids differently."

What you choose to do today could reverberate throughout your family tree for a very, very long time. But you *must* act. The longer you wait, the more time the poison has to take hold of your life.

And if I had to guess, I'd say you've been waiting for at least three reasons: denial about your impact as a parent; the fear of being found out; and an unspoken belief that God might be far too much like your dad.

So let's consider—and put to rest—each of those issues.

PART II
TO FORGIVE YOUR FATHER

CHAPTER 8

THE INCREDIBLE, INESTIMABLE IMPACT OF A FATHER

"The most life-changing, significant, and meaningful work you will ever do is in your home."

The news article "The Delinquents: A Spate of Rhino Killings" recounts a disturbing discovery:

In South Africa's Pilanesberg Park, rhinos were thriving until an unknown killer began stalking them. Thirty-nine rhinos, 10 percent of the population in the park, were killed.

The killings clearly weren't the work of poachers. The rhinos' horns hadn't been touched. The park rangers began conducting an investigation. Their first findings led them to believe that if they were to round up the usual suspects, they'd need a pretty large holding pen.

That's because the prime suspects were not humans,

but elephants. It turned out that young male elephants were behind the murders of Pilanesberg's rhinos.

Why would they do it? Well, like juvenile delinquents, they had grown up without role models.[4]

The report goes on to reveal that several years earlier, a large group of adult male elephants had been put down because they couldn't be transported to the new park because of their size. As they studied the younger elephants, a pattern emerged: The murderous teenage elephants suffered from an excess of testosterone. Because these teenage elephants had no role models, they didn't know how to act or what they were supposed to do.

Consequently, the younger, testosterone-filled elephants ran wild, causing all kinds of problems and killing the rhinos. To solve the problem, researchers brought in adult male elephants. When the bigger elephants arrived, they established a new hierarchy, sometimes even sparring with the younger elephants to discourage them from being sexually active. The younger elephants soon understood how they were supposed to behave. The rhino killings stopped.

A father's importance transcends even the boundaries of species.

If we profess to believe that God created the world, and that how He created it was just as good as He said it was at its inception, then we ought to understand the centrality of a father's role in his child's life.

WHEN FATHERS FAIL

Because I experienced it, lived it, filmed it, and then wrote about it, I truly believe most men have no idea of the significant and lifelong impact they have on their children. If fathers actually understood their inestimable impact on their sons and daughters, I would hope they'd all act quite differently, and the world would become a different, better place.

Just look at the social issues of our time that can be the result of a distracted, distant, or deserting dad: early sexual activity, teenage pregnancy, a growing inmate population, drug addictions, gang associations, and the list could go on.

While at a youth prison, a chaplain once told me, "You know, John, these kids aren't bad kids."

I raised an eyebrow at him, and he could probably hear my unspoken thought: *But they're in prison.*

He repeated himself and finished his thought: "These kids aren't bad kids. They just don't know how to be good because they didn't have a father."

I nodded in agreement. I could understand that. *There but for the grace of God certainly go I.*

After watching the short-film version of *The Father Effect*, another prison chaplain essentially told me the same thing: "John, you say in your film that nine out of ten people have a father wound. In prison, it's twelve out of ten."

I didn't doubt him. The sorrow I'd felt for myself as a young man, and the sorrow I'd more recently felt for my father, turned into sorrow for the young men and women who were serving time because a father had failed to give them his time. Looking back, I often think about how I easily could have been one of those young kids in prison. After all, my father did prison time, and that particular form of a generational curse could have imprisoned me, too. On many occasions, I was just one bad decision away from being where they were. I just got lucky, I guess, or God provided just enough grace to guide me away from the bad decisions I could have made.

Behind those prison walls, in a place that was all too reminiscent of a childhood I'd tried to forget, I thought about time. The teenagers behind those bars had all the time in the world to think about who they were, but I imagine that they never took the time to think about who they could be.

They were captive elephants who didn't have a clue as to how they were supposed to act in the real world.

THEY CAN'T BE WHAT THEY DON'T KNOW

In *The Father Effect* film, pastor and author Paul Cole says, "Men struggle at being good fathers because they don't know what a good father's supposed to be. They haven't been taught. You can only give what you have. Most of us, as men, not having been taught properly, just do what we kind of think is right. 'It seems kind of right, but I'm not sure if it's right. Well, heck with it! I don't have time to do anything else. Let's do this.'"

I interviewed Craig, a father who was unknowingly failing his daughter because he was subconsciously still trying to seek affirmation from his father. He was a successful product manager who would often volunteer his time at his church's youth ministry by listening to their struggles and counseling them as best he could. So he was surely surprised when his daughter finally told him about a string of abusive relationships she'd been in. After Craig received encouragement from a coworker he had confided in about his father wound, he and his family began seeing a counselor.

In one of the sessions, every finger seemed to point to Craig as the source of his daughter's inability to find a nonabusive boyfriend. Any man in his situation can imagine his shock. He was confident he wasn't the source, particularly because he considered himself a good counselor for other kids. How could he miss something so devastating in his own child's life?

But the facts won out: Craig was successful at work, and that meant he was seldom home. His daughter didn't have a present and engaged role model for how a good man should act. Craig *was* a good man, but he just wasn't home. Therefore, his daughter sought attention elsewhere.

In time, Craig realized the depth of his influence on his daughter. He also began to understand his father wound and how he was inadvertently re-creating the family dynamics in which he'd grown up. Because Craig's father had been an aloof businessman, Craig modeled the same thing for his family. He believed the lie that fatherhood mostly just equals provision and worldly success.

Craig later told me of another conversation he had with his coworker that he'll never forget when he was asked, "If there was one thing you wish your dad had done differently, what would it have been?"

Craig's answer was simple: "I wish he would've said, 'I'm proud of you.'"

Craig then waved an arm at his thousand-acre ranch and his multiple luxury cars. "You see this? I did this to get my dad's approval, and to this day I have never heard those words, 'I'm proud of you, son.'"

Maybe it's too simple to think that if Craig's dad had said, "I'm proud of you," then Craig wouldn't have worked so hard for so little, and then he would have been home more, and then his daughter would have had the role model she needed, and then she wouldn't have been in those abusive relationships. But generational curses don't have to be complex. They just need to be ended.

Craig fell prey to becoming the kind of father he likely believed he wasn't, but thank God for His intervening work of opening Craig's eyes to how central his presence was to his daughter's life.

Some fathers wound with their detachment. Others wound with their absence.

ABSENCE MAKES THE HEART GROW A HOLE

One could argue that even applying the word *dad* to a voluntarily absent father is incorrect. At best, when *dad* is used to describe an absent father, it just means "biological contributor." I'd argue that an absent father is no father at all. If they've vacated their responsibilities as a father, why should they get to hold on to the title?

Stephanie's father falls under this definition. When she was four, her parents divorced and her father moved to a different state. She would see him only during the summer. But around the time she turned twelve, the summer visits stopped and she never saw her father again. Without even that small amount of influence—Stephanie described her dad as kind, giving, and funny—a void opened within her.

She dropped out of school and left her home at sixteen. To make money, she started dancing in strip clubs. In "a very dark life of doing drugs, living at night, and sleeping during the day," Stephanie was a topless dancer from her late teen to early adult years. But thankfully, Stephanie related to me that God told her to pick up a Bible one day and just start reading. Her life drastically changed as she read God's Word. She soon left the club, which meant also losing all of her friends.

Although Stephanie doesn't blame her father for her decisions, she understands how his absence contributed to her motivations to make those decisions: "When there's not that male influence there...there's this void and there's this hunger for that male attention. And I definitely needed that and wanted that in my life."

When I heard those words, I wondered about the background of the other dancers she'd known. I asked her to guess "what percentage of the women that you danced with didn't have an engaged, involved father in their lives."

She replied, "Ninety percent plus."

I shouldn't have been shocked, but I still was.

After leaving that lifestyle, Stephanie began a ministry to help women likewise walk away from the exotic dancing industry. Because I knew of her involvement in that necessary ministry, I asked her what most of the women she rescues struggle with.

She didn't hesitate: "Self-worth and how they view themselves. Their father is a huge part of that, and when it's missing they fill that void with attention. And it's the negative attention of, 'He's looking at me. He's giving me attention.

He's giving me love. He tells me I'm pretty,' and it's a false sense of identity... Seeing who you are and your identity, you look back at your father."

I'm grateful for Stephanie and the work she's accomplished, and I'm thankful that her life was so changed by God that He's used her to do the same in others' lives. Stephanie told me that when she talks to women who are just like she was, she tells them, "The old has passed away. All becomes new from here on out. What you thought you were is not what you are, but you are what God made you to be. And *He's* your Father. He's the one you look at for your identity."

I wish everyone could understand this way of thinking.

THE EMPTY MODEL HOME

A father's physical absence or lack of affirmation can wound a child forever, but so, too, can his inability to be a father because it wasn't modeled for him while he was growing up. Often, being a "bad dad" doesn't mean such men are bad people. Rather, it's as if they've been asked to renovate a house but they have to craft the tools to do so themselves. There's a reason why this notion of a lack of modeling—my dad couldn't give me what he didn't have—keeps popping up. It's truth.

Phil was an incredibly talented and charismatic young man who came from a long line of athletes, some of whom had played for the NFL. I met him through a mutual connection at a men's summit in Los Angeles, and he graciously agreed to be filmed for *The Father Effect*.

Phil shared that his father was then a homeless drug

addict whom he hadn't seen in nine years. In a telling story about how a father indelibly imprints himself onto his son whether he actually tries to do so or not, Phil told me, "I remember drinking certain drinks because I remember seeing my dad drink those drinks. There was no other reason. I didn't like the taste, but I remember the images of my dad carrying that bottle in his hand, and that was the only reason I chose that drink out of all the drinks in the liquor store. It was because that's what my dad drank."

When I asked Phil what he wished his dad would have done differently, I loved his answer, even though I was saddened by it:

I wish my dad would have shown me how to be a man, what it meant to just be a respectable man. I wish he would have taught me how to deal with women, how to treat women. I wish he would have taught me how to be different than all the other guys. When all the other guys were out there sleeping around and having sex, I wish he would have taught me about purity and respecting myself. I wish he would have taught me not to curse, not to use profanity, because I was real good at it by the time I was in fourth grade. I wish he would have taught me self-control.

He concluded with his most revealing statement: "All the things that I know now that I so want to teach my kids, I wish my dad would have taught me."

Such a man isn't handed the tools he needs to be the dad he longs to be. He can learn these things through books, conferences, sermons, and talking to other men, but he may always feel like a fake when he tries to enact something different in his parenting that he's learned from such sources. There's no teacher quite like a real and engaged father. That kind of modeling imprints what it means to be a man and a dad onto a young man's heart. When a man acts as a result of what's been positively modeled for him, he acts courageously and doubtlessly.

He doesn't feel like an impostor. He feels like a man mirroring the man he wants to be.

"ONE OR TWO OUT OF A HUNDRED"

The epidemic of rejected boys turning into angry or confused men has likely infected a much broader population than any of us would want to believe.

Gordon Dalbey speaks to men all over the country about this plight. I was fortunate and glad to have interviewed him for *The Father Effect*. Dalbey has written a number of books, including *Sons of the Father: Healing the Father-Wound in Men Today*. An anecdote from that book reveals the unfortunate depth and breadth of the father effect:

> Late in the fall of 1991, shortly before becoming a father myself, I asked a conference of 350 fathers, "When your first child was born, did your father reach out to you with support, encouragement, or helpful advice?"
>
> I paused as a strange hush settled over the men. "Maybe," I suggested, "your dad...said something like, 'It's a little scary at first, but hang in there and you'll be

doing fine before long' or 'Make sure your wife gets a break from the stress and rests once in a while'?"

The hush stirred to nervous shifting as one...then two more...and finally, a total of five hands went up. *Only five out of three hundred and fifty?*

Stunned, I resolved to test this statistic at my other conferences around the country. Everywhere, the proportion came out roughly the same: one or two out of a hundred.[5]

Of the men Dalbey spoke to, only 1 to 2 percent received any form of encouragement after their firstborn arrived. That's sad and shocking, but maybe it shouldn't be so surprising. If Dalbey had interviewed these men's fathers, I imagine his proportion would have been the same—and maybe even lower.

Their fathers couldn't give them what they never had themselves.

Men, consider for a moment your experience as an adult son. Has your dad ever given you meaningful, in-depth advice about being a husband and a father? Or about how to properly handle finances? Or what to do when faced with a dicey ethical situation at your job?

If he has—ever—consider yourself one of the blessed, lucky few. You're one of the two men who would have cautiously held their hands up in Dalbey's story. That's not to say that your father wound isn't gaping, but your father at least made an attempt to be a dad at some point in your life. Apparently, few men can say the same.

It would seem to me that most fathers enact what was tacitly passed down to them. The sons of the fatherless default to thinking and believing, *I learned how to get by in life on my own. My son can do the same. That's what makes a man a man.*

There's another name for that kind of thinking: the generational curse.

But unfortunately, dads don't suffer only from that curse or from what their fathers couldn't provide to them. They must also fight against the way our culture views men.

CHAPTER 9

DON'T DRINK THE COOL-AID

"Every man wants to be seen as the hero."

As a child, my favorite Saturday morning cartoon was *Popeye*. As a teenager, my favorite movies were *Rocky* and *The Godfather*—maybe I thought my dad would show up in the background. In my early twenties, I gravitated toward films that always had a hero who could kick butt and exact revenge.

Looking back, it's easy to see that the men I admired were, above all, strong. Unsurprisingly, they were the John Wayne types: "Talk low, talk slow, and don't say too much." They needed only their fists, their guns, or their usurped power to prove their manliness. Even if I didn't know it back then, that's who I wanted to be, and TV and movies fed me a constant stream of tough men I could idolize. If I didn't have a dad at home, at least I could find a few men to look up to.

Most of the kids I grew up with were like me: raised more by TV dads than any man in the home. In Section 8 housing, even seeing a father was a rarity. Unfortunately, the ones I did see weren't the best examples of a good father. On the unique occasion that I made a friend who had a good dad, I gravitated toward them. I wanted to be around that father— or any father figure, for that matter. I desperately longed for a man to show me how life was supposed to be done and what a good father was like.

I was jealous of my friends with dads, no matter how bad they were. During my twelfth-grade year, my two best friends and I had a drunken argument about whose life was the worst. These two friends both had dads, but both dads were alcoholics. (How surprising, then, that our argument was a drunken one.) They complained about how poorly their dads treated them and how they never seemed to take an interest in their lives. Of course, I replied by cussing and yelling at them in a drunken stupor, "At least you two have a dad! I don't care how bad he is. You have a dad."

I was so sure I had the worst life, but I think culture had convinced me that I was pretty much like most of my friends. Even the dads who were still in my friends' homes weren't really dads. They were there but not *there*. Most of my friends didn't have dads, but I still felt alone because no one else's dad had committed suicide.

During high school and college, as my connections to others broadened and I met more and more new people, real dads became much more prevalent. Maybe it was because I became more involved in sports and other extracurricular activities and I'd see involved dads in the stands, cheering their sons on. Whatever the reason, I realized how different I truly was. I was Rocky with no coach in his corner. I was the Godfather with no consigliere.

I had to wait for the only male heroes in my home to come on every Thursday night at eight.

OF HEROES AND HOMERS

When John Eldredge spoke about heroes and Homers in *The Father Effect* film, I was amazed that I'd never picked up on that dichotomy before.

Images of masculinity in the media are kind of crazy-making because they go down these two really different tracks. You get the Bruce Willis, übertough, *Die Hard* guys able to jump off buildings, take a couple of hits to the leg, and still get the bad guys. [They have] this incredible power, strength—the superathletes, the guys who can do the triathlons and the Ironmans—all of that. But then you also get in the media that most dads are kind of idiots. You get the Homer Simpsons. You get the caricatures of men as kind of bungling fools.

Every man wants to be seen as the hero. Every man fears he's the idiot, and so: Don't do anything that could expose yourself, that you are the idiot. I don't want to be Homer Simpson. I want to be Superman. I want to be the amazing guy. We'll do everything we can to find a way to prove that we're amazing, and we'll do everything we can to hide any possible flaws in us.

A divorced friend of mine vowed he would never marry another woman who didn't have a good father. He told me that his ex-wife had grown up without a dad. As a result, she had an unrealistic view of what a father should be. She'd devised a fantasy image of a Superman dad that my friend could never live up to—that no one could live up to. Before he'd even met her, he was already failing her expectations.

I don't know from what sources she cobbled together her definition of a father and husband, but I wouldn't be surprised if the emptiness created by her father wound led her on a search for an idealized dad, which popular culture is adept at portraying—at least when it's not showing men as bumbling idiots.

Barring the rare outliers on TV and in film, the dual ways the media portray fathers are so pervasive that we subtly accept them as fact: *This must just be the way dads are.* Or we shrug off the power of media.

Dr. Meg Meeker knows better: "I think the media has a huge role to play in beating up dads. Dads say, 'Yeah, but that's just TV.' But look at television, look at movies, listen to the music that our kids listen to, and there is not a smart dad to be found. Dads are portrayed in the media, which our kids are watching three, four, five, six hours a day, as dumb. Kids believe their dads are dumb. While we may say, 'Yeah, that's just TV,' make no mistake: Our kids are listening to this."

I didn't realize it at the time, but I was often subconsciously comparing the men in these shows and films to the man I thought—had hoped—my dad was.

Following his death, I chased his memory, desperately wanting to discover a man I wished I could have known better. I longed for him as my hero, but as I learned more about his hard life, he became far more human than what I'd dreamed of while growing up as an innocent, naive little boy. The reality of who my father was could never live up to the Superman father who lived on the movie screen of my mind. My journey toward forgiving him began when I started to reconcile my hero worship with his humanity.

As I learned about his life—his abandonment at sixteen to live alone in the Big Easy, his constant battles with depression, his ultimate decision to stop his pain—I wanted to run away from him as fast as I'd once longed to run toward him. I couldn't handle the reality of his life. I wanted to forget all the bad and remember only the good. I wanted to look at that picture of him holding me as a child and forget that it was taken in front of a prison.

Funny thing was, one of my biggest struggles in counseling was trying to remember any real physical moments with my dad. I was distraught over the fact that I couldn't recall even a single moment of doing something with my dad, like fishing or playing catch. Even though I'd had an idealized version of my father in my head for so long, in my counselor's office I realized that what I thought had happened and what had really happened were two very different things. And because I didn't want to face the truth—that my dad really had abandoned me, my brothers, and my mom so long ago—I sank into denial about his effect on my life.

Because I chose to deny his humanity and reject his title as *my* father, I sought role models elsewhere. I bought into every definition of a man that the world offered.

MAN OF THE WORLD

As I went about my life, I constantly looked for ways to prove to others that I was a man. I don't think this search was a conscious decision; rather, it was my heart trying to protect itself. *If I can show how much of a man I am, then other people won't think anything's wrong with me.* I tried to fill the hole in my heart with everything the world told me I absolutely had to have. I had learned that a "real man" has power, money, success, and women, and he's chiefly defined by his ability to drink beer. In fact, the beer commercials made it seem like drinking beer made all those other things instantly appear. I could get on board with that, so I did.

But above all, I sought success and money. At the time, those two things were synonymous to me. If I could earn enough money (which was always just a little more than what I thought my friends or coworkers made), then I'd know I was successful. And if I was successful, then I'd know I was a real man. Money was the easiest barometer to measure my manliness. If I didn't have enough money, I considered myself a failure.

Looking back, it's no wonder I was depressed so often.

Because money was my focus and the measure of my manhood, I made a good amount for a time. But this led to a more devastating issue: entitlement. Because I earned the income to provide for my family by working so hard, I justified going out and getting drunk anytime I chose. It was my personal reward for a job well done (and further proof that I was a real man).

And the worst thing about entitlement is that it doesn't affect just one area of your life. It bleeds into everything.

Looking back, it's a miracle my family stuck with me.

On the day I heard John Eldredge talk about men in the media, I realized three truths: (1) I had been a Homer for a long, long time; (2) and I could never be a hero; (3) but I could be what a real man, husband, and father should be, not according to what the world said, but according to how the Bible leads.

TO REVEAL THE INNER MAN

Yet it seemed like most of the men I knew couldn't admit to being Homers either. We were all too proud. Or, at least with some of the guys at my church, we were all too scared to admit to one another that our carefully created Christian facades were one near-crisis away from burning to the ground. I don't blame these men for acting that way. After all, it was the way I acted, too.

In some ways, I blame accepted church culture. Pastor Brady Boyd perfectly captured my thoughts about church during this time of my life:

> We look around at the church culture that we're a part of, and we look at these men who seem to have it all together—because all of us are wearing these church masks. The culture in most churches is, "Everyone is

behaving well," but you know what's going on in your heart, and you know you don't measure up to that. I am not the man that they think I am. That's the first thought that comes to these men...But I'm afraid for them to find out.

So, because I'm afraid for them to find out the real person, I'm going to control my relationships, and I'm never going to really be vulnerable and transparent. So we learn to live with this goofy church mask on, pretending that everything is okay when we know it's not. But we can't imagine us telling the truth, because then we would be exposed, so we start posing. I think that's the culture most of us find ourselves in in the local church.

The safest place to fail should be the local church. The safest place to be truthful should be the local church, when, in fact, it's the most dangerous place to fail in most cases, and it's the most dangerous place to tell the truth because the penalty for telling the truth in most churches is: You get ostracized. You get labels put on you. "So you're fifty years old and struggling with porn? What the heck? What are you doing? What's happening? You can't kick this?"

So, instead of me being transparent with someone and asking for help, I just go deeper. I just push deeper, and I put on a more and more complex church mask.

I used to wear many masks, and I especially put on one before going to church. For attending a place that preaches truth, honesty, and transparency, that's not a healthy habit. But, from my personal experience and the hundreds of discussions I've had with other Christian men, men in today's church aren't offered much help *by the church.*

For instance, I once spoke to a men's ministry leader of a major Christian retailer who told me they didn't have a dedicated men's ministry division until after the movie *Courageous* was released in 2011. It was only then that they saw the need to bring in a full-time men's ministry division leader. When I asked why his company had waited so long to do so, his answer stunned me, and I've never forgotten it: "We mirror the church and what the church is doing and focused on." I couldn't believe it. The church wasn't focused on men until *Courageous?* Didn't a group of men *start* the church? (I didn't bring that up in our conversation.)

I've always believed that strong fathers lead to strong families who make up strong churches. The real change the church needs should begin in the single hearts of each of its men. However, it certainly wouldn't hurt for male pastors to begin getting real about their own struggles as Christian men, husbands, and fathers. Some pastors are great at doing this, but I believe they're few and far between. And while I can't even pretend to know the pressure, responsibilities, and spiritual warfare that pastors face on a daily basis, I do know that men will drop their "goofy church masks" when the pastor drops his first.

Still, while I think the church can and should take great strides toward strengthening men, the chief responsibility of every man—and particularly those who are fathers—is to assess himself and stop blaming anyone else.

For me, the sad truth is that I was afraid of looking within. I feared what I might find. I feared more that I wouldn't be able to deal with whatever resided there. I'd buried it for so long, had drowned it in so much drink, and had covered it up with as much cash as I could earn that I was certain a monster of epic proportions awaited me. I seldom looked at myself in a mirror because I knew the monster would be looking back. I feared that once I began the descent into my heart, I wouldn't be able to find my way back from that dark abyss. I felt that I was too far gone to come back home. I was a man prepared to eat pig slop (see Luke 15:11–32).

But I desperately wanted to change.

Again, like a surgeon, John Eldredge cut to the heart of my story:

> Society does not encourage this kind of openness, a kind of honesty, among men. I mean, sadly, in the church, we don't encourage discussion of brokenness. We're scared of it—feels like it might be somehow diminishing what God has done for us, or we just don't know how to deal with it. Some guy opens up his brokenness and everybody freezes and goes, "Holy cow, this guy is a mess. We've got to get him to a counselor." When, in fact, every man you meet is broken inside. You just don't get through this world without taking those wounds.

Men need to realize their woundedness, lay down their egos, and seek the right kind of help. Sometimes that means doing what our culture has unfortunately deemed as less than manly. Years ago, I felt the same way. When I finally knew that I needed more help than just reading books about fatherlessness or going to more church services, I told my wife not to tell *anyone* that I was going to see a counselor. Why? Because "real men" don't see counselors. They don't need to talk about their feelings or how they were hurt or abandoned as a child. They certainly don't need to pay for the experience. They should just buck up and shut up.

The negative stigma of counseling, which has gratefully lessened over the decades, still exists, largely because our culture perpetuates the idea that it's unmanly to be vulnerable. Essentially, I think we all tend to believe that John Wayne would never step foot in a counselor's office. There's even a phrase to prove this point: Those who have post-traumatic stress disorder and refuse to talk about their experiences are said to have "the John Wayne syndrome."[6] If all men want to be heroes, all men want to be John Wayne. So we hurt alone and dig our silos of depression even deeper.

But freedom from that pain is on the other side of laying down our definitions of what a real man is.

THE PROBLEM WITH MEN

One stereotype of men that's often portrayed on film and TV is that men can't commit. As a man, I'm a little offended by that, but I also know that it's true, or at least it has been in my life. I could argue that I committed myself pretty heavily to...myself. I committed to drinking as much and as often as I could. I committed myself to working as long as I could to earn as much as I could. I committed to whatever I thought was best for me.

But when it came to committing to someone other than myself? To say yes to my wife and children over my feelings of entitlement? To deny myself and take up a cross and follow God?

Uh-uh. No way. That was too hard. That would demand too much of my already battered soul. I'd endured so much as a child. I'd involuntarily given up my dad. Why should I have to give up anything else for anyone?

I realize now that a man's basic problem when it comes to his father wound isn't commitment; it's the act that commitment requires: surrender. To commit to anything requires surrendering some part of one's will, and guys just don't want to do that—probably because we don't think we have to. We approach it almost like a business deal where we vainly believe we can finagle the best angle where all parties (but mostly us) get the best end of the deal. We cajole, challenge, and rationalize with others so that we don't have to give up much to earn what we want from any relationship. We do this in our friendships with other men, in our marriages, and in our relationships with God. That's what I did. I could talk a good game, but the fruit of my actions always bore witness to the root of my problem. I couldn't commit because I couldn't surrender.

John Wayne doesn't surrender, right?

When I speak to men today and share the same ideas this book covers, many of them nod their heads in agreement. They follow right along with me for a majority of the talk—until I get to surrendering. When a word like *surrender* gets tossed around, crickets start filling in the silence. I fear that men just can't handle the word or its vast implications in their lives. Honestly, it drives me mad that men don't re-

DON'T DRINK THE COOL-AID

spond, even though I should know better because I used to be that way and I can *still* be that way.

I work hard to ensure that these men understand how fully surrendering my will to God was essential to healing my father wound. I want to drill it into their heads that surrender isn't a sign of weakness but a badge of honor. As a man, the world says you cannot be weak. God says that He is made strong in your weakness. Do not believe the lies of this world.

We ought to applaud when a fellow man admits that he can't do life on his own and needs God's guidance. If men would just pause and ask themselves, *So, how's your life been going since you've tried to solve all your problems on your own?* and make an honest assessment of their lives to that point, I imagine they might finally realize how much help they really need.

When men can't get honest enough with themselves to understand their deep need for total surrender, they'll continue living an unfulfilled life full of regrets. Their only friend will be their puffed-up yet fragile ego. The men I speak to seem to want to hold on to that lesser version of being a man instead of opting for the more challenging yet freeing path of becoming the husband, father, and son God means for them to be. And all because they fail to understand that "I surrender all" isn't just a hymn lyric; it's a prescription for abundant living.

After all, the man we're supposed to emulate lived His life in full surrender to God's will and ultimately surrendered His life. He had every reason in the world to exercise His will, but for the greater good of others, He gave up everything. This is the bar that has been set for men, a God who became a man so that all Homers could one day become their children's heroes through faith, trust, and surrender to God.

I know what you may be thinking, and it may be the final question holding you back from forgiving your dad: *How can I trust a God who I'm not so sure isn't just another version of my absent dad?*

CHAPTER 10

FATHER GOD

"God was there; it's just that He was far away—like my dad was."

Why do the children of the fatherless have such a difficult time surrendering to God?

The answer should be apparent.

How many times does God refer to Himself as "Father" in the Bible? He is called "Father" 15 times in the Old Testament, more than 165 times in the Gospels, and over 40 times in the Pauline Epistles.[7]

One of the most well-known prayers of all time begins, "Our Father in heaven" (Matt. 6:9). Christians have long been taught the world over about the Father, the Son, and the Holy Spirit. The imagery of God as a father cannot be escaped.

And this tends to make the fatherless lean two very different ways:

1. I'll allow God to father me, to replace the earthly father I lost or never had. (John Eldredge's book *Fathered by God: Learning What Your Dad Could Never Teach You* is an excellent resource on this topic, and should be required reading for all, particularly the fatherless.)
2. If God is like my earthly father, I want nothing to do with Him.

If I had to guess, most children of the fatherless fall squarely into the second camp.

I certainly did.

JUST LIKE DAD

Somewhere along the way—maybe it was from TV or the example set by my friends' fathers—I thought that obtaining love from your father meant you had to earn it. I didn't have a word for it back then, but I now know that this is called "performance-based love." Whether a father actually loves his child based on their performance isn't the point. If the child *feels* that he or she must act right to be acceptable to Dad, then that relationship is tainted with performance-based love.

And that kind of relationship translates all too easily to a child's relationship with God.

For years, I saw God as a dictator focused solely on discipline and punishment for my inevitable mistakes, like not telling my mom about finding my dad's gun. I felt that I could never measure up to God's perfect standards. I thought that no matter what I did, it would never be good enough for God to love me.

If I experienced major issues or decided life wasn't going the way I wanted it to, I believed it was because I wasn't close enough to God. I thought that I should be reading my Bible more, or praying more. I saw God as a sort of bank teller. Whatever I put in was what I'd eventually receive, maybe with a few dollars of interest.

Even when I felt somewhat closer to God, or when life seemed to be going well for a time, I'd cautiously wait for the other shoe to drop. In the back of my mind during those good times, I'd hesitantly think, *Well, something bad's going to happen sooner or later. Guess I just need to enjoy this until reality busts down my front door again.*

At other times, I just felt that God had been removed from my life. He existed, but I wasn't sure He really cared about what I was doing—unless I was doing something wrong. Plus, I laid the blame for my father's death squarely on God's shoulders. If God really loved me, He wouldn't have let my father take his own life. He would have used His powers to prevent that from happening so I wouldn't get hurt.

For what it's worth, that's not God. That's a broken, fatherless boy's poor theology in the midst of intense personal pain.

Unfortunately, much of what I'd gathered from my father's friends and the churches I attended while growing up didn't help sway my distorted view of God. He was all about what I wasn't supposed to do. Even as an adult, guilt would cause me to believe that God was already disappointed with me, which would then lead me to believe that I might as well keep sinning. He couldn't become more disappointed, right?

I used this terrible theology as my own free pass. I would

do wrong to convince myself of my guilt, and in my guilt I would continue to do wrong. I somehow convinced myself that I was a good Christian—at least an okay Christian—but I held fast to a weak view of God. In my journey toward becoming the man God longed for me to be, He would have to work to dislodge and replace my poor theology.

Because I'm adept at compartmentalizing my life, I had long separated my father wound from my beliefs about God. But through filming *The Father Effect*, I learned how intricately tied together they really were. I didn't recognize then that my father wound had affected my very soul.

THE GOD-FATHER EFFECT

Show me a person with a father wound who hasn't adequately dealt with it, and I'll reveal to you a person who feels removed from God. I wrote "feels" on purpose. God is always near, especially to the brokenhearted (see Ps. 34:18), and if the fatherless aren't among the most brokenhearted, I don't know who else is.

For better or worse, your view of God was likely highly influenced by your view of your dad. As a child, and maybe still as an adult, God the Father was all too often just a loftier version of your father: stern, distant, and forced to love you, if He even acknowledged you.

Phil, a youth pastor, was well aware of how his nonexistent relationship with his father discolored his relationship with God:

Because of the disconnect—the distance between me and my dad emotionally, spiritually—I didn't really have that with God. I didn't even know it was possible. So, whenever the word *father* was spoken, my mind would go right to my father. I could not separate the two.

The first time a pastor...suggested to say, "I love You, Father," was weird. I couldn't say it. I literally could not get the words out of my mouth. I had to force the words out. After I said it, I had to think about what I just said. It did not make sense to me. I couldn't make the connection that I could actually say and mean that "I love You, Father," because of the bitterness that I had toward the person who played the role of the father in my life.

The connection between our fathers and our Father is so intertwined that I've often wondered how many atheists have absent fathers. Through the lens of the father effect, their lack of belief in a higher power makes sense. If Dad is gone, God must be, too. But, of course, atheists aren't the only ones who have to wrestle with the lifelong ramifications of an absent father.

Stephanie, the former exotic dancer, saw God as far removed from her because her dad was just as distant: "I just found God to be somewhere out there, somewhere. No one that was personal. No one that was there, really. That's how I viewed my dad for a long time because he wasn't near to me. He was living in another city. God was there; it's just that He was far away—like my dad was."

There's something powerful, and powerfully condemning, about these memories. What kind of power does a father truly hold? The power to shape his child's perception of God. Is there any greater power than that? Whether by word or deed (or the lack thereof), men tend to hold such power loosely. It's more likely that we just don't want to believe such a heavy burden sits across our shoulders, but this is the cross all fathers ought to bear.

When reading Phil's and Stephanie's stories, did you feel a kinship? If you're unsure how deeply your father wound has cut into your spiritual life, pause for a moment and ask yourself these questions:

- *When I envision God, does He look like my father?*
- *When I describe God, could I also be describing my dad?*
- *When I hear about God as a Father, do feelings about my earthly father arise?*

For a father-wound sufferer to enjoy a healthy relationship with God, the father effect must be dealt with. It doesn't have to be "solved," and it doesn't have to be placed on a to-do list as if it's just another life goal to achieve someday. Rather, dealing with your father's effect on your relationship with God means acknowledging your hurt and taking real steps toward forgiveness.

I'm a living testament that God will meet you on that pathway.

THROUGH MY FATHER'S EYES

I hope the way God drastically changed my life through healing my father wound is evident. It was an arduous, challenging, but rewarding experience, and one that I wish I had started decades earlier. At the very least, I wish I hadn't thrown away so many years when my daughters were young.

Now that I'm older and hopefully a little bit wiser, I have a new and more expansive view of fathering that takes into account how my girls may see me as their role model for God.

Even writing that sentence makes me shudder at such a title. Fathers bear heavy burdens, and showing our children how God loves them may be our chief responsibility in this life. But doing so doesn't mean a father has to be perfect (good luck if you want to try!). Rather, I believe it begins with a simple, daily task: Always try to see your kids through God's eyes—the same way God looks at you.

It helps to have a healthy and correct view of God's vision. At the very least, know and believe that He loves you regardless of how bad—or how good—you are. That's why it's called unconditional love. Realize the truths of Romans 8:1 and 8:38–39: If you're in Christ, you are not condemned; and *nothing* can separate you from the love of God. Taken together, those are powerful facts about your existence as a beloved child of God.

Because of my relationship with God, the way I view fathering today is radically different from the way I viewed it previously. I'm sure that at times He shakes his head at me and wonders, *Really? Did John just do that? Again? After all I've taught him?* But then He quickly grants me more grace and mercy than I deserve. He loves me regardless—regardless of my sin, my laziness, my selfishness, my arrogance, my cowardice, my achievements, my fears—the list is endless, but the fact remains: God loves me regardless.

Children need the same from their earthly fathers.

Fathers can be shocked, confused, or frustrated when their children fail to meet their expectations. But a godly father shouldn't use that as an opportunity for goading, demeaning, or sarcasm. Rather, he should consider how God would relate to him about the same issue and then likewise relate to his child in the same way. Of course, that means dealing with detrimental issues and facing the truth of any situation, but that also means exuding unconditional love throughout the process.

I believe God allows us to experience struggles so that we might draw closer to Him. In a similar way, when hard times face your children, they draw closer to you if you've established a healthy relationship with them. When those hard times inevitably arrive, whether for you or your children, let them remind you of who your real Father is. Realize that just as we hope our children can trust us and find security in our presence, we can all trust God to be our best Father. I always tell my girls that they need to have a close relationship with God because I won't always be near when tough times descend into their lives. Ultimately, their Father God is the only one they can fully and forever trust, the only one who will never leave them or forsake them.

Still today, with my daughters in their teens and soon to leave our house for good, it's easy to forget they're just kids who are learning the ropes, which causes me to grant them more grace. But that also makes me think about myself: Even though I've been a dad for almost two decades, I'm also still learning the ropes. I'm not always going to get this "godly male role model" thing right. But I give myself grace in that respect, and God is faithful to grant the same to us as we struggle *together* to be the kind of people and the kind of family He longs for us to be.

God is patient with me, always.

God is proud of me, always.

God loves me, always.

May that be said of how you parent your children as well.

THE GOAL

When I think about the kind of father I want to be, I think about Neal Jeffrey's dad, who bore the burden of fatherhood well:

He was my hero...He always prayed for us...He'd write me a letter. My dad was a letter writer. He always referred to me as "Honorable #1 Son" 'cause I was his first son. "Dear Honorable #1 Son, just wanted you to know I mentioned your name to the Father this morning. Love, Daddy-O."...He spoke truth into us.

Just by his life we thought, *This is how a man does life.* How does a man love a woman? Well, every boy needs to know that. I know how it ought to be done 'cause I had a man who did it. I watched him do it. I watched him love my mom. I realized, *You know what? I want to be like my dad, who did life well.* His marriage was good—wasn't perfect—but it was a good, strong marriage. He loved my mom, honored my mom until the day he died, raised us kids...I realized that's who I want to be and how I want to live my life.

It makes me realize every day I want to live my life in such a way as a dad that when my son passes my life, I pray he sees something in me. He wants to be just like his dad. When my girls have been raised in such a way by me and have seen me treat their mom in such a way that those girls feel like, *You know what? I'm not going to settle for any man unless he's like my dad and treats me the way I've seen my dad treat my mom.*

Neal Jeffrey's father was a godly role model. His life revealed what it meant to be a man to his "Honorable #1 Son."

As the apostle Paul asked the early Christians in 1 Corinthians 11:1 to "follow my example, as I follow the example of Christ," a father ought to ask his child to follow him as he follows God. The truth is that a son or a daughter will do that regardless of where the father leads. Because they know no better, they will live what's been modeled for them when it comes to the things of God. And while they may rebel against a father's modeling, either away from or toward God, the fact remains: A child's earliest model for God is their earthly father.

Jeffrey said what I hope my daughters will one day say of me: "I was following my dad, and I ended up following who he was following, which was Jesus." For my daughters to be able to say that about me, I had to learn to trust a God who revels in being a father. Instead of seeing God as someone who'd left me just as my dad had, I had to see God as the father who ran to his wayward son "while he was still a long way off" (Luke 15:20).

I had to experience deep forgiveness before granting it.

CHAPTER 11

THE HEALING POWER OF FORGIVENESS

"He that cannot forgive others breaks the bridge over which he must pass himself; for every man has need to be forgiven."
—*Lord Herbert* [8]

I was forty-one years old when I first admitted having a father wound. For thirty years, I'd lived and suffered without knowing why so much of my life had felt wrong and out of control. I had no idea my dad's suicide had affected me so deeply. Because he chose to leave me when I was barely a teenager, I didn't understand that anything necessarily had to be "dealt with." I thought my life was mostly normal. So I dealt with my unfounded pain the only way I knew how: by *not* dealing with it.

But then February 20, 2009, happened, and I finally surrendered my life to God. During a counseling session a couple of months later, God revealed a question to me that would truly begin my journey toward understanding my father and myself. This question was the key to many long-locked doors in my heart. The words were so pointed and meaningful that I felt as if God were giving me answers to all of my lifelong questions—in the form of a question: "How can you be so angry, bitter, and resentful toward a man who didn't know how to be a father?"

As if the clouds parted, I instantly connected with my dad. I couldn't expect him to give what he didn't have. The empathy that one question engendered in me led to my being able to forgive him, even in his absence. My life was irrevocably changed. I learned that forgiveness frees the fatherless from past pain so that their futures can be filled with love and hope.

Maybe it's cliché to say, but I left the counseling session and was sure the sky had turned bluer. The grass *was* greener. Scales had fallen from my eyes. What had seemed so cloudy and murky to me became clearer than anything I'd ever seen before. It was as if I'd been looking at life through broken, cracked, dirty glasses for most of my existence, and through that defining question, God gave me a new pair so I could better view Him, my dad, my family, myself, and my world.

My rational mind had known about the impact of my father's fatherlessness for a while, but it wasn't until that day that my heart agreed with my head. Through one simple question, God transplanted me into my father's life. In one moment, God granted me an empathetic response to my suffering that I'd never experienced before.

Keith, the friend whose singular question on a golf course one day forever altered my life, said it well in a clip that didn't make it into the documentary:

My dad was one of eleven children. I called them "the Herd." They didn't get a lot of nurturing. Let's just say it like that. It was more about keeping them in line...So, he didn't get [nurturing]. The Lord showed me, "How could he give it? It wasn't in there!"...How can I be angry with somebody who couldn't give me what they didn't possess?

Phil, a youth pastor, put it bluntly: "My dad never knew how to be a father. He never knew how to be a man." After sharing how his dad's father had died when his dad was only two and how his dad's stepfather had also died a few years later, Phil said what I came to understand about my own dad: "He really never had a chance."

How *could* I be so angry about my dad's inability to give me what he'd never received himself? It was like asking for a mansion from a man who'd only ever earned a living wage.

And even though I didn't realize it on that day, I later saw God's fingerprints on why He'd chosen February 20, 2009, as the day to awaken me to what I'd been numb to for so long. Four decades and one year earlier to the day, on February 20, 1968, when I was just a month old, my dad had reported to prison for his first day as an inmate.

On the forty-first anniversary of when my father lost his freedom, I had just begun to gain mine.

THE ROAD LESS TRAVELED

Forgiving your father for the wounds he's willingly and unwillingly inflicted upon you is hard. In fact, it might be one of the most difficult journeys of your life. There are so many diversions off the pathway toward forgiveness:

- Shouldn't he be the one to ask for forgiveness first?
- I don't even know how to contact him anymore.
- He's not alive.
- He never cared. Why should I?
- If I told you what he did to us, you'd be shocked.

These are all valid reasons for not forgiving the man who was supposed to be your foundation, but that doesn't get you off the hook of forgiveness!

When I began seeking to forgive my father, the most enticing diversion was the fact that he wasn't around anymore. How could I forgive someone who'd already passed away? Subconsciously, I'm sure I used this excuse to dismiss myself from dealing with my father wound for decades. And if I ever thought about forgiving him postmortem, I'd just recall how absent he was in our lives even when he was living. I didn't give him a break.

Someone once asked me, "Is it tougher to live with a father wound inflicted by a father who's still alive or by a father who's dead?" After much thought about my experience and those of the people I'd interviewed, I said, "Living with a dad who's still alive. That's a constant reminder of the wound." My dad was dead, and there was hard-fought closure, but I believe it's more difficult to forgive a still-living father who's wounded his child. Still, choosing to forgive *anyone* is a battle against yourself.

When God showed me that forgiveness was necessary for my growth and the impact I was having on my children, I listened. I had to face the conflicting truths that I'd been deeply hurt *and* that I'd have to forgive the one who had caused that pain. Consequently, I faced emotional, physical, and spiritual battles all along the road toward forgiving my father.

Emotionally, I constantly and arrogantly believed I could handle my problems by myself, which led to self-isolation. Or I'd believe something was really wrong with me, which led to depression, shame, *and* self-isolation. Physically, the stress of essentially leading a double life at church, at home, and then at work, compounded by my drinking habits and expanding waistline, aged me faster than I should have been aging. I'm sure these were just ramifications of the real issue: a spiritual battle for my soul.

I grew up in church hearing the phrase "spiritual warfare," but I never believed it actually happened until I began seeking forgiveness for my dad with God's help. I was angering the devil and he didn't like it. He kept reminding me that I was unworthy, shameful, and ought to be regretful. He whispered that I should just "man up and do it on your own, John." But thank God for His protection and guidance.

I learned that forgiveness is valid only if it's total forgiveness. I learned that if a hint of bitterness or resentment still resided in my heart or mind, I hadn't completely forgiven my father. When God allowed me to find forgiveness for my father, it was unconditional. After that moment, I never wondered whether I'd truly forgiven him. I knew I had.

As *The Father Effect* film came together and I kept hearing more and more incredible stories, it reaffirmed to me just how powerful and life-changing forgiveness is. I wish everyone could experience it. So many have been freed from the burden of fatherlessness because they've chosen to take that incredibly hard but necessary step to forgive their fathers.

Unforgiveness is a prison you choose to live in. Forgiving

the person who's hurt you the most may be the single act that's preventing you from experiencing total freedom and healing and truly becoming the person God created you to be. But where should you even begin?

ADMIT YOU HAVE A WOUND

The first step to healing is admitting you're wounded. Most men deny their father wounds because they don't want to deal with the reality of what's happened in their lives. They know it can become very emotional, both in anger and in tears, and they simply don't want to go there. (John Wayne doesn't cry, right?)

Gordon Dalbey says in *The Father Effect*, "Recognize that your dad didn't give you what you needed 'cause he never got it. He never had it to give. You gotta forgive your dad. You gotta pray, 'Jesus, show me my dad the way You see him.' But have a box of Kleenex on hand. I always say, 'A little boy cries from his father's wounds.' Dad hurt you. You cried. A real man cries *for* his father's wounds."

By admitting that you're wounded, you're facing your deepest issue head-on, stepping up to be a man, and accepting the fact that you have a problem. Acknowledging your woundedness gets you past the roadblock of denial.

In my documentary, John Eldredge speaks the truth of what's required of a man who's tired of pretending everything's okay:

The journey towards an authentic masculinity and the journey towards authentic brotherhood involves a willingness to quit faking it, to just go, "Look, I'm done with the poser. I'm sick of that guy. It's the false self. It's the mask I put on to the world. I'm just sick of it. I'm done with that life. I don't want to be that guy anymore." Setting that stuff down, and also beginning to experience some genuine healing of the inner brokenness—that opens up this phenomenal world of friendship and connection and band of brothers that guys crave and is available. And it's available in Christianity like it's available nowhere else.

God may allow circumstances to conspire against you—which is really just another way of saying that your sins will catch up to you—so that you come to the end of yourself. When you get to the end of the road you've created for yourself, that's when God can show you a better path. But you have to be realistic about where you are and where you're headed, and you have to be sick about the prospect of going down that road any farther.

You must admit your wound before continuing. After all, how can you ask forgiveness for a wound that doesn't exist?

INVITE GOD TO HELP YOU

I couldn't just admit that my dad had hurt me. Anyone who had an inkling of my past knew that. Even though I wasn't open about my father and his impact on my life, it was easy to tell that something was off in my life. But it's not enough to just agree that you've been wounded. You have to reach out for help, and that first reach may sometimes be the longest and the most difficult.

You were created to depend on God, and He longs to help you. But you also have to want to help yourself. For instance, have you ever really looked at *The Creation of Adam*, Michelangelo's famous painting on the ceiling of the Sistine Chapel? Adam sits in a reclined position, a depiction of humankind's natural proclivity toward passivity. But God is stretching, rushing, and reaching out with all His might to reach Adam. And yet their fingers don't meet in the painting. Even Adam's finger is slightly bent downward, while God's is fully extended. All Adam has to do to touch the living God is raise his finger just a few degrees.

This is an all-too-appropriate depiction of the state in which most men find themselves. God is nearer than you think. With a word of submission, He will rush in to guide your path. Asking God for help is cracking open the door of your heart just an inch so that He can change you from head to toe. Just as Jesus said during the Sermon on the Mount:

Ask and it will be given to you; seek and you will find; knock and the door will be opened to you. For everyone who asks receives; the one who seeks finds; and to the one who knocks, the door will be opened.

Which of you, if your son asks for bread, will give him a stone? Or if he asks for a fish, will give him a snake? If you, then, though you are evil, know how to give good gifts to your children, how much more will your Father in heaven give good gifts to those who ask him! So in everything, do to others what you would have them do to you, for this sums up the Law and the Prophets. (Matthew 7:7–12)

God's love is stronger than the chains that bind you. God's love can break the generational curse in your lifetime. God's love reveals a true Father. It's fitting that Jesus talks about sons and fathers in that sermon.

When I finally confessed my need for God and fully surrendered my life to Him, I began to experience what John Eldredge put so well: "Deal with the internal pain [and] you won't need the medication anymore." When I sought God's help, He lifted this worn-out workaholic alcoholic from the dead-end street he was walking and placed him on the path to life. But He didn't leave me alone to struggle.

SEEK COUNSEL OR ACCOUNTABILITY

I knew that I needed to tell someone about my change, and I told any man who would listen (and eventually any woman, as I realized the father effect harmed them, too), but in sharing about my newfound freedom, I knew I needed a confidant. That's when I sought Dr. Tom, and as you already know, his insights led me to finally forgive my father.

Don't forget: You were also created to live in community with others. Through trusted and knowledgeable men and women, you ought to seek counsel and accountability for your decision to fully and finally forgive your father. By doing so, you'll stand to gain insight, help, and direction in your life. Those who give you counsel can help you translate what you're hearing from God into practical next steps. They can caution you to proceed slowly. And they can congratulate you after overcoming a fearful part of the process.

Don't make the mistake of believing what you might have formerly thought about not needing a counselor or community. Don't isolate yourself because you think no one really knows or cares how you feel. Someone does, and God will lead you to the right person at the right time. You cannot make the journey of father forgiveness alone—the burden is too heavy for just your shoulders. Find trusted friends with whom you can share where you are and where you're hoping to go. And I can't speak highly enough about spending the time and money necessary to connect with a qualified Christian counselor with whom you can meet face-to-face at least once a month.

Now that you've admitted your wound, invited God to help you, and sought counsel and accountability, you need to do one more thing.

FORGIVE YOUR FATHER

That's an easy sentence to read. With only three words, it seems so simple. You want to nod your head in agreement. After reading this far, forgiving your father makes sense—in your head. But as Andrew Bennett, a British politician, famously said, "The longest journey you will ever take is the eighteen inches from your head to your heart."

If that's true, and I believe it is, I needed three decades to travel eighteen inches!

I don't know what it is about a man's wiring, but we live in our heads almost all the time. Try as we might, we can't escape our next thoughts because they come in a never-ending torrent. And when those stray thoughts of *Yeah, my dad* did *hurt me* flow through that nonstop downpour, they're quickly washed away by the next deluge: *What's for dinner? Will I make partner? I need a drink.*

So you can pass by the sentence "Forgive your father" and think nothing of it. You can read Christian books that tell you how good and right and freeing it is to forgive your father, but that could still have little effect. You have to allow the profound, resounding, challenging truth of that statement to bore a hole past your mind and deep into the recesses of your heart.

What would it mean if you truly forgave your father?

If you have a hard time fathoming that, consider these stories from *The Father Effect.*

"I WAS AT PEACE"

At the time of our recording, Dennis was eighty-four years old, and his father wound had pulsed with every beat of his heart for as long as he could remember. At least, that is, until Dennis chose to forgive his father.

> Instead of thinking of the negative things [about my father], I started thinking about the positive things about him, which, as I stated, he's always provided. We always had food on our table, clothes on our back, and those things were all positive. 'Cause I know there are a lot of fathers that didn't provide for their families. My father did. Even though he didn't say, "I love you," he was providing for us.

And I kept thinking along those lines, and I thought about how young he was when I was born. He was about twenty-six years old is all. And he just didn't know. He just didn't know how to express love, I don't think. He did with my mother. There was no problem there at all. He loved my mother. I heard him tell her many, many times, but he couldn't do it with us.

So I began to feel a little bit guilty about this, and I said to myself, "I forgive you." And I did it from the heart, and then I asked God to forgive me for even thinking that way, you know. All those years of resentment were gone. I didn't have 'em anymore. I went to bed that night, [and] as I laid there, and I went to sleep, . . . I was at peace.

Dennis's story showed me that it's never too late to forgive your father. Even if you're a grandfather who's harbored resentment toward your dad for as long as you can remember, you can still choose to forgive him for what he was unable to give you. You can still be the hero who breaks the cycle of the generational curse so that it doesn't have to keep affecting your children and grandchildren.

"THE BEST THING I'VE EVER DONE"

Larry is a hulking fitness expert. To see Larry is to see what most men would aspire to be if they could regularly go to the gym for longer than a month. Yet even men like Larry suffer from father wounds.

In 1969, *60 Minutes* interviewed Larry's father, Irv, because he was in a treatment center for an addiction to gambling. Back then, that center was unique, which was why the producers wanted to share stories from within its walls. And because Irv was just as outgoing and charismatic as Larry, he was a natural choice for a feature.

Larry showed me this interview, which briefly told of Irv's addiction and its negative effects on his life and family. In fact, they even interviewed a skinny teen with a big Afro, Larry, who openly talked about "this character named Irv." He alternated between great fondness and even adoration of his father and severe disappointment in and frustration with him.

As the show ends, Morley Safer asks Irv something along the lines of, "What do you think your odds of beating your addiction are?" I don't recall Irv's answer, but *60 Minutes* did a follow-up show ten years later. The first scene is an interview with Irv—in prison.

When Larry was an adult, he had a maddening conversation with his dad where he tried to get Irv to see the ramifications of his addiction. His father responded, "Larry, you are my boy, and I have never done anything to hurt you." Irv failed to see how his absence had truly and deeply hurt his son.

But when Irv was diagnosed with cancer years later, Larry was still his son and brought his father to Dallas to take care of him. Irv had been given only a few months to live. Larry knew that his window of opportunity to forgive his father for a lifetime of fatherlessness was quickly closing.

But the day he chose to finally and forever forgive his father didn't turn out as he'd expected:

I remember getting a call from the VA hospital. I was friends with one of the nurses there, and I said, "Just let me know what's going on at all times."

She called me and she said, "You better get down here. I don't think you're gonna have another chance to say good-bye to your dad."

So I immediately hustle down. Then I get to his hospital bed, and my dad is completely passed out. I grabbed his hand. I knew I needed to say it then. I couldn't even repeat the words that I said. I just know it was full of love and forgiveness and wishing him the best.

When I turned around, a nurse had walked into the room while I was talking to my dad. She was just full of tears. She said, "I just didn't want to interrupt you to tell you that he passed away an hour earlier."

I said, "You know what? I didn't do that for him. I did that for me," and I did. It was important for me to truly forgive him in my heart. It's the best thing I've ever done.

Larry told me that had he not found forgiveness for his father, he would not be the man he is today. From what I know, he's a man who helps others, has the strength and peace to share such a hard story, and seeks to make a difference in the lives of all he meets by the example he sets with his life.

Unforgiveness is a poison that will ultimately rot you from within. Even worse, that poison slowly and subtly seeps out and affects your every relationship. You might think that choosing not to forgive your father will hurt him, as if your act of defiance will somehow cause him the kind of pain you've long experienced. But that's not the truth. Choosing unforgiveness hurts you and the ones you love. Many times, a dad doesn't even know he needs to be forgiven. The forgiveness is *for you* so you'll no longer live in the prison of unforgiveness.

Beyond our need to forgive for the sake of others and ourselves, God calls us to forgive freely and often. The Bible often reminds us to "forgive as the Lord forgave you" (Col. 3:13); and, while I don't know about you, I know that the Lord has had to forgive me for *a ton*. Who am I to forgive anyone any less?

Forgiveness is a powerful thing. It freed me from the chains of anger, bitterness, and resentment. It relieved the burden of guilt, shame, and unworthiness that I carried for most of my life. I found forgiveness, but what I also received was a second chance to be the man, husband, and dad I was meant to be. Choosing to forgive my father has been the most challenging road I've ever traveled, but I wouldn't trade it for anything, and I would do it all again. What I've learned has helped me change my legacy as a father, made me a better father, and has forever changed my life.

My hope is that you, too, will take that step.

Forgiving your father could be the greatest gift you ever give—and receive.

PART III

TO BE THE MAN GOD CREATED YOU TO BE

CHAPTER 12

A REAL FATHER, A REAL HUSBAND

"The best thing a father can do for his children is love their mother."

As soon as I'd hear my office door crack open, I'd leap from my chair, march to the opening door, shoo my children away, and yell down the hall, "You know I'm trying to work! What are you doing letting them come up here to interrupt me?"

I cringe now to think of the volume and tone I once used with my wife. My children were young before I fully committed myself to God, during what I call my BS (Before Surrender) years. For more times than I'd care to admit publicly, when they'd scamper into my office as I was working and interrupt me, I would become annoyed and yell at my wife because of their intrusion. I was getting work done, earning a living, and putting a roof over their heads and food in their mouths. I didn't have time to give to my kids. I was too busy providing.

Is there a lie that men have believed more?

I'm ashamed that this was the man I once was. I could rationalize my outbursts in so many ways, but the truth was that my selfishness ruled our house. During that time in my life, my children were young, with such short attention spans that they needed only a few minutes of my time before they'd scamper off to the next thing they wanted to do. If I could have allowed just a moment of intrusion, I likely would have made their day.

But I was the one acting like a child.

HUSBANDS CAN'T AFFORD TO BE SELFISH

We're all born selfish. That's the hand each of us has been dealt since the fall of man in the garden of Eden. Then, as babies, we're (hopefully) given attention, as if we're the center of the universe. Our parents meet our needs. Early on, we're given no inclination that being selfish is wrong.

As we learn to speak, we learn that oft-repeated mantra of the toddler: "Mine! Mine! Mine!" We're forced to learn how to share our toys and how to play well with others. We cry because we don't understand why the world no longer revolves around our every need.

Some of us require time that extends long into adulthood to learn that lesson.

I was a selfish man for too long, and I still struggle with selfishness today. Early on in my marriage, I thought I could continue to live as if I were single. Because I wanted to, I kept hanging out with my friends. I seldom if ever considered how that made my wife feel. I doubt I asked for permission. I just went because I felt like I'd earned it. In my mind, I was my own man and no one else—even my wife—was going to tell me what to do. We argued on multiple occasions when I wanted to go out and she wanted me to stay home. I'd "win" because I'd just leave. Today I know how good God is because my wife weathered those moments of my idiocy!

We're all selfish, but I think men are a special kind of selfish. And I don't mean that in a good way. We have a difficult time looking to the needs of others over our own. Even Christian men forget Philippians 2:3: "Do nothing out of selfish ambition or vain conceit. Rather, in humility value others above yourselves." For reasons beyond the scope of this book, men have a hard time exercising humility—especially in their marriages.

I needed years to realize that I'd made a commitment to my wife to be one flesh, and not just in the traditional Christian idea of "one flesh," sexually speaking. I needed to understand that we're a team, where we both always work for the benefit of the other because that benefits the team, because both are one. (God's arithmetic isn't rational!) To place her needs before mine, I had to learn how to die to self every day. Unfortunately, dying to self doesn't seem to get easier with practice.

To this day, the most difficult prayer for me to say is, "God, Your will be done—not mine," especially when I'm so sure that *my* will is God's will. As you've read, I long struggled to trust God because I felt just as abandoned by Him as by my earthly father. But asking God for His will to be done requires a deep trust that God's will actually is much better than your man-made decisions. You must trust that dying to self and choosing to serve others is *better* than constantly addressing your own desires and wants. I promise: You will reap incredible relational benefits with your wife if you begin dying to self on a daily basis.

When I don't feel like trusting God, I remind myself of the latter part of Hebrews 13:5: "God has said, 'Never will I leave you; never will I forsake you.'" Knowing that God has always been there for me, that He's here for me right now, and that He will always be there for me in the future reassures my doubting heart that all will be well, even if life doesn't go according to my plan. When I can lay down *my* plans, my hands are then open to accept His. Truly believing that God wants His best for my family and me has changed my life and how I approach every day I have left to live. Even though selfishness still slithers like a snake into my world, I now long to be a selfless husband and father.

Dying to self in the home truly begins with addressing how a husband relates to his wife.

THE EXAMPLE YOU SET

When I was a young father, I wasn't just modeling a bad dad; I was also modeling a bad husband. For a father of three daughters, that could have been a substantial mistake. I'll leave it to the insightful counselors and psychologists to tell you about "family of origin" issues, such as when a child recreates her or his parents' marriage, and often unwillingly and subconsciously so. But the heavy truth I finally began to understand was that what I modeled in every way I related to my wife was what my girls would deem "normal male and husband behavior" for the rest of their lives.

And yes, I count my blessings that my girls were too young to notice much about our marriage while I was living like an idiot. At least I hope that's the case.

When my daughters heard me arguing with their mom, or saw me storm off to be by myself whenever life got hard, or saw me react to conflict in a verbally or physically aggressive manner, they could reasonably have considered my actions to be average-guy behavior. In fact, they might even have come to *expect* such behavior and subconsciously seek it out. This is one reason why so many marriages seem to be mirrored reflections of a spouse's parents' marriage. The generational curse strikes again!

The responsibility to model what you want to see in your children doesn't lie solely with Dad. How my wife treats me will be the model for how my daughters will eventually treat their own husbands in time. But I would argue that the father sets the tone for modeling helpful, loving, godly relationships.

Dr. Meeker opened my eyes to the importance of modeling when you're a father of girls:

> Modeling is very, very important and particularly for a little girl watching how her dad treats her mother. It's not just how he treats her. I mean, that's extremely important. It's interesting because dads will often be kind of rough with their wives. They may yell at their wives. They may swear at their wives but then turn to their daughter and treat her very differently. Well, that doesn't sit with a kid—with a daughter, particularly. So it's not only important how you treat your daughter, but how your daughter sees you treat other women: [your wife], [your] own mother, [your] sister.

I now relate to my wife in a dramatically different way while at home. These days, I gladly show love and affection for my wife in front of my kids as much as possible (despite their protests) because as a husband and father, I want to give them the most tremendous and influential example I can of loving a wife and mother.

We are not perfect by any means, but my kids have a new picture of what a loving husband looks like. Hopefully, they now know beyond a shadow of a doubt what a husband and wife are supposed to be like and that their mom and dad love each other incredibly. Now, their new "normal" ought to set quite a high bar for any would-be future suitors.

Pastor and author Paul Cole said, "The best thing a father can do for his children is love their mother. For a child to see his father love their mother, something happens in that child…that centers their life."

Fathers, your daughter learns how she should be treated by a man by watching how you treat your wife and the other women in your life. Show her what it looks like to be loved, respected, and cherished.

PROOF THAT MODELING WORKS

I don't share the following to toot my own horn. In fact, I'd hazard a guess that what you're about to read is more influenced by *The Father Effect* documentary and the untold hours that my wife spent talking to my daughters, but I'd like to believe that some of the work God has accomplished in my life over the last decade also contributed to these words.

My teenage daughters each wrote their definitions of "a real man."

Syd (17)

A man does not just go to church once a week, but is a man of God. Love God first. Lead me and my family to a life full of Christ. Be honest, humble, and genuine. Respect me and my boundaries, and encourage me and push me to reach my goals.

Brooke (15)

a man
a man is someone who owns up to their own mistakes
a man is someone who can have an actual conversation
a man is someone who has morals and viewpoints
a man is someone who knows what to do in weird situations
a man is someone who doesn't talk down to others to make himself look better
a man is someone who is selfless
a man is someone who never degrades women
a man is someone who is capable of love
a man is someone who can control their temper
and above all a man is someone who has faith in God and does the right thing

Ellie (10)

I think a man should be godly and prays with his kids every night. He should ask them what they would like him to pray for them about. You need to know when your children are hav-

ing struggles. Also, a man should be respectful and kind. They should open doors for girls, offer their seats, and don't be dirty. They should also be really respectful to their wife. They also need to have one-on-one time with the kids. Talk to them about their day and take them somewhere. And that is all a man needs to be a great man.

Maybe I should have just let them write this chapter. Praise God, they get it. Whatever men they may meet or one day marry, I have confidence that they'll be good guys. Certainly, none of those guys will ever be good enough for any of my girls, but at least my girls have high expectations for the way they'll be treated by men.

This doesn't happen by accident. All husbands can learn how to die to self and how to better model what a real man looks like in the home. Men: To be the kind of father you wish you had, be the kind of husband your wife has only dreamed about.

WHAT IF I'M NO LONGER A SPOUSE?

Because my dad left my family through death and not divorce, I've hesitated to talk about divorce. Even though divorce is an epidemic in our country that has ravaged millions of families, my experience of fatherlessness and abandonment was significantly different from the experiences of those who've suffered the ramifications of divorce. In other words, I imagine it was easier for me to forgive my absent father than it is for a child of divorce to forgive their still-living father. My experience with divorce has all been secondhand, through friends and documentary interviews.

That said, it's important for divorced parents to attempt to model healthy parenting and respect for each other.

For divorced dads, you may not technically be a husband anymore, but you will always have responsibilities as a father. And because you can't divorce your role as a father from your role as your child's mother's at-least-onetime partner, you must work to respect her as best you can for the sake of your children.

I have to imagine that to die to self in such circumstances may be the most challenging request God places in your life, but consider the kind of picture of God's love you're painting when you choose to love and respect your ex when all the world expects you to act differently. Consider the light in which your kids will see you when you opt for kindness over meanness, patience over frustration, and respect over disdain. Even if you're no longer in your child's life on a daily basis, you're still modeling for him or her what a man ought to be—so be a good one.

For divorced moms, you're still a model as well, and relating to your ex in a healthy manner is important for your children to see. However, as single moms often retain custody, it's also important that you relieve yourself of the burden of feeling that you must be your child's mom and dad. You're only one person, and you were never created to fulfill the role of a father anyway. You will exhaust yourself and likely frustrate your child at the same time.

Regardless, you can't allow that void to go unfilled. Every child needs some kind of healthy male influence. Take advantage of opportunities for your child to receive that. I know this can be a very difficult thing to do, especially for women who have been deeply hurt by men, but you *must* ask men of character for help. Ask your pastor, a male friend, an uncle, a grandfather, or a coach to come over and spend time with your son or daughter once a month or once a week. Offer a free meal in return. (What man can turn down a free meal?) They don't have to spend money on your child. They just need to spend time with them.

This is extremely important because your child needs to see how a positive, godly man acts, talks, and lives life. If your children don't have this example, they likely will look to the world for an example—and that's the last place you want them searching. If that happens, they'll likely have a warped view of what a man is supposed to be.

Although I believe the church needs to do a better job of helping single moms (and single dads) fill in the gaps, there are some great organizations that help single women find healthy male mentors for their children:

- **The Mentoring Project:** www.thementoringproject.org
- **Koz Kids:** www.kidsoutdoorzone.com
- **Big Brothers Big Sisters of America:** www.bbbs.org
- **New Commandment Men's Ministries:** www.newcommandment.org
- **A Father's Walk:** www.afatherswalk.org

Some of these organizations work through the local church, too. Find out what organizations are available in your area. Perform your due diligence on who's behind the group and what they offer. Talk to other women who have joined the organization or have used the organization's services.

You don't have to go through an organization, but doing so can certainly help quicken the process as they'll likely already have vetted, willing men ready to mentor your child as a godly role model. The point is to simply take a step toward finding such a model for your children.

THE COUNSEL THEY NEED (AND YOU, TOO)

I'm a huge advocate for Christian counselors. Dr. Tom was key in helping me find healing from my father wound and understanding my own behavior. I tell people he was the Aaron to my Moses. He was my encourager and my accountability. He was my challenger who never hesitated to call me out on all the ways I'd tried to hide from myself and others. I don't know if I would be where I am today if it weren't for Dr. Tom. I wish I had seen someone like him many years ago to help me process my struggles.

If you're a single mom or a divorced dad, take your child to a Christian counselor. There are things your child will not tell you that he or she would tell a trusted professional. As an eleven-year-old and into my teen years, I didn't want to burden my mom with any of my issues because I knew her plate was already full just trying to be a single mom to three boys. So I shouldered my heavy issues alone and wound up carrying that weight for most of my life.

Your child needs someone who knows how to help them and can provide a safe place where they can unburden themselves. As a divorced dad or a single mom, you might think you know how to help them, but you don't, and I would hazard to guess that the issues you may be working through—

or may still need to work through—could warrant seeing a Christian counselor of your own.

To find a qualified counselor for you and your child, ask your church or close Christian friends for recommendations. If that doesn't provide any leads, search online for Christian counselors in your area. Again, do your vetting homework while conducting the selection process. After your child (or you) has begun seeing a counselor, be patient. The work they do, and the internal work your child may be doing as well, takes time. But if you have a qualified and helpful counselor, the benefits will be well worth the wait.

MEN: LOVE YOUR WIVES AS CHRIST LOVED THE CHURCH

For men with absent fathers who have children of their own, the second step to take after forgiving your father is to love your wife well (even if she's your ex-wife!). In Ephesians 5:25, Paul reminds us, "Husbands, love your wives, just as Christ loved the church and gave himself up for her." When truly considered and honestly lived out, that's a tall order: daily surrender of self in its most blatant form.

Loving your wife well means loving your children well, too. And when you take a journey of father forgiveness as a married man, your wife will be traveling her own path as well—which might be a journey of just forgiving her own father or even of forgiving *you*. Words can't express my gratitude to my wife for sticking with me through so many hard years, and I'm thrilled that in the following chapter she shares how *The Father Effect* affected her, our marriage, and our children.

CHAPTER 13

GO FOR THE ASSIST

A Word from Michelle Finch, John's Wife

"You are the most important teacher your kids will ever have. Teach them well."

Our oldest daughter, Sydney, is passionate about basketball. Even at an early age, she truly understood the game. As point guard, her ability to strategize yielded her the most success. While most players couldn't control their urge to go for the shot themselves—even at the varsity level—Syd prided herself on the assist.

Despite being the top scorer on her high school team that year, on rides home we typically heard, "Did you see that pass I had to Alex!?" She became a great three-point shooter during high school, which earned her the most accolades from other players and coaches, but she remained most proud of her ability to get the ball into the hands of a player more strategically placed for the score.

She never minded putting aside her personal victories in order to achieve more success for the team.

Before I really understood the special role that John plays in the lives of my girls, I was simply in the business of "meeting needs." We always seemed to be short on time and long on our collective needs, so I just got things done and moved as fast as possible to the next thing on our family's list. Without a doubt, I got things done more efficiently than John, so it made the most sense to me to be the one to take care of whatever our girls needed when they needed it. It wasn't that I didn't want John to have the "win" if he helped the girls solve a problem or surprised one of them with something I knew would help them get through a tough day; I just took care of things myself because that was easier.

But as John filmed *The Father Effect*, I learned just as much about myself and my parenting as John did. I realized I seldom went for the assist. I always wanted to be the one who scored. Now I understand that my girls need to know they can depend on their dad to protect them, to defend them, and sometimes just to brighten their day. They need him in a way that I could never fulfill. So I try to emulate Sydney's winning strategy of taking the shot when it makes sense but *always* looking for the assist.

For example, as an infant, our youngest daughter had a health issue that required her to be sedated for a procedure where she had to be perfectly still for thirty minutes while inside a huge tube that blared loud and scary noises. When she recently had a follow-up MRI as a ten-year-old, she didn't require sedation, although the process was certainly intimidating for her (as I think it would be for most of us).

Before I recognized that her dad is truly whom she looks

to for protection, I would have just scheduled the appointment and taken care of it. I wouldn't have seen the need to take us both away from work to check this item off our list. However, with my newfound desire to make assists rather than points, I found a day when we could both be there. (Someone had to take care of the paperwork!)

Our daughter loved having us both there, but she was definitely on edge, and I could tell that she was anxious and scared. When it was finally time for the procedure, only one parent was allowed to go into the room with her. I nudged John to head back.

I know all my girls look to their father for certain things I can't give them. While I'm the only parent who can talk to them about boys from a female perspective and show them how to be confident women, John's the only parent who can instill a certain confidence and strength within them that everything is going to be okay. There's a uniqueness to a father's capability of making his children—and particularly his daughters—feel valued, cherished, safe, and secure.

During her procedure, what our youngest daughter needed most was the feeling of security and protection she could get only from her dad.

YOUR FAMILY IS YOUR TEAM

In moments like those, I realized more than ever that John and I were the coaches of our family team. We needed to learn each other's strengths, including how each of our girls uniquely needed us or responded to us, and we needed to allow each other to play to those strengths in our parenting.

When Sydney was younger, she got frustrated with some of the other players for simply not sharing her vision on the court. They were great at getting into position under the basket for her to pass the ball or boxing out for a rebound. But when they found themselves with the ball after a steal and tried to dribble it back down to their basket, the other team would often steal the ball back. As the girls on the team got older and gained hard-won experience, they learned not to get caught up in the moment but rather to get the ball back to the point guard, go to their proper positions, and have everyone prepared for what each player did best.

In watching them begin to gel as a team, I witnessed how important it was to their success that everyone played their position. To win, everyone had to play to her strengths and know where her teammates worked best.

On our parenting team, I'm definitely the point guard. I like to believe that I have the most accurate vision of all that's going on with the girls at any given time—and with teenage girls, there's *always* a lot going on! I've learned that I can't be mad at John for not having the same "court vision" I have. He's more focused on the now and the immediate future, like a post player readying himself for a rebound. Because we've experienced it time and again, I know our team can be most successful when I "read the court" for him and help him adapt accordingly.

For example, when Sydney was in ninth grade, she wanted to spend the night at a friend's house—on a school night. John's immediate response was, "Nope! It's a school night." He was still stuck in the rule book of elementary-age kids, but we were dealing with a teenager, and there's certainly a need to gradually release control as they gain independence. I reminded him that when it came to school responsibilities, no one was harder on Syd than she was on herself. I suggested that she really needed the comfort of a friend that night due to a struggle she was having.

Whether he wanted to face it or not, our daughters were growing up. He was going to have to adapt and change his "old rules" for these new chapters. But *together* we read the court of our home and found success with our team.

FOR WIVES OF THE WOUNDED

I wrote about parenting first because that's what comes to mind when many mothers think about their father-wounded husbands: *If only my husband would change, then our kids could have the kind of dad they've been missing.* But be warned: In the hopes of having a better father for your children, don't try to change your husband.

No matter how hard you try, you can't change your husband. You may be able to amend his ways for a time, but real, deep, lasting change—the type of change brought about by something like forgiving his absent father—happens only at God's leading and your husband's surrender. Don't tire yourself out in trying to accomplish that work on God's behalf. Certainly, pray for your husband and his needs, but don't shoulder the burden of trying to change his heart. You can't, and you'll only frustrate yourself and your husband if you make it your mission to force father forgiveness onto him.

Rather than seeking what you're powerless to change, do the one thing you *can* do: understand.

Although I knew John had gravely suffered from the loss

of his dad, I had no idea that he carried the consequences of insecurity and fear long into his adulthood—and our marriage. Like him, I never connected his actions with his unhealed father wound.

In hindsight, everything's clear. Situations and conversations that drew reactions I just didn't understand can be completely explained now that I know what he was feeling for all those years. But that's exactly the problem for most wives, isn't it?

We don't know what our husbands are feeling because it usually isn't in their nature to share it with us. Now that I know what drives my husband to certain behaviors, I don't take it as personally. This really helps me to not react as strongly when something he does upsets me. And a deeper understanding of his pain—and his forgiveness—provides me with more knowledgeable ways to pray for him.

The Father Effect documentary has already changed so many, and I will remain forever grateful to God for our journey in making it, for the sole reason that He used that time to bring John and me closer together and to help us become better parents.

Through John's journey, I learned so much that changed not only my marriage but also my parenting, and even my view of the world in general. Here is what I now know to be true:

GOD ABSOLUTELY CAN HEAL OUR DEEPEST WOUNDS.

Of course, we have to surrender our own will, stop trying to fix things ourselves, and be willing to do the hard work that's required, but I'm telling you: My husband's heart was most certainly changed. When we try to fix ourselves, make progress, and make changes to our behavior, there is simply nothing like God coming in, focusing our perspective, and providing true healing from past wounds and mistakes.

JUST BECAUSE MY HUSBAND IS WRONG DOESN'T MEAN I'M RIGHT.

I realized that no matter how big of a mistake one partner makes, it doesn't automatically mean that the other partner is completely blameless. I may not have the same faults my husband has, but I definitely have others, and I can't expect him to walk around taking the blame for every kink in our relationship. Even when I know John is in the wrong, I can still be the one to apologize first, ask what is wrong, and really listen.

JUST BECAUSE I'M BETTER AT SOMETHING DOESN'T MEAN I SHOULD TAKE OVER.

In general, women are good at multitasking. It really may drive us crazy when we watch our husbands do things in a way that seems completely inefficient to us. It used to make me insane when John went to the grocery store and brought home all sorts of wacky things. He bought the wrong brands, got tons of junk, and completely forgot the main thing I asked him to stop for! I used to rant and become angry about it, but now I just laugh it off. I really am thankful for his shopping "attempts."

139

MY CHILDREN NEED THEIR DAD TO DO CERTAIN THINGS, AND I SHOULD STAY OUT OF THE WAY.

In my experience, mom skills are different from dad skills. We may feel that we know more about our kids and can handle daily parenting situations better than our husbands, but we need to just let that go. My girls always had a different standard for their dad anyway. What would have been completely unacceptable for me to do—feed them grilled cheese sandwiches for three days straight—was completely fine when I left town and they were with Dad. Instead of trying to control how he does things, I need to just let him do things his "dad way."

I'd like to think we've had more wins than losses in this game we call parenting. We're not perfect parents by any means, but we're on the same team now—unlike the many years we spent acting as competitors.

Not long after God radically changed John's life, John asked me, "Do you have any regrets?"

I paused, and then I said, "Yes, I do have a regret. I wish the John Finch I know today was the John Finch I had for the first fourteen years of our marriage." It was bittersweet, but it was the truth.

I'd be lying if I didn't admit that I've wondered about what our lives would have been like if John had found forgiveness for his dad much earlier in our marriage. However, I'm thankful and blessed that he eventually did.

Some never do.

CHAPTER 14

DADDY'S LITTLE GIRLS LOST

"If a daughter knows that she has her dad's love, life makes sense."

I couldn't help but laugh when I saw what she was doing. As I stood in front of the TV in our living room, flailing my arms and legs around like a madman, my four-year-old daughter imitated my every move as I mimicked the exercise coach on the screen.

She couldn't stop herself from laughing either. I couldn't blame her. Gravity had taken its toll on this spring-turned-into-fall chicken, and I imagine that anyone seeing me gyrate out of rhythm to the music would have been laughing. But there's something precious, wonderful, and holy about a four-year-old's unbridled laughter.

Then she did something so telling. After accomplishing the exercise at hand (with incredible strength, dexterity, and endurance, mind you), I stopped to take a swig of water and wipe the sweat off my forehead. Before reluctantly returning to exercising, I looked back at my daughter.

She took a long drink from her sippy cup and dabbed her forehead with her blanket.

I can't be any more blunt: *Everything* a father does defines what a man is to his daughter. You are setting the standard as a man, husband, and father by which your daughter will measure every other man, husband, and father. I did not know or understand this truth when I first became a dad, or even when I became a father the second and third times. I learned of this deep but so apparent truth only during the filming of *The Father Effect.*

I had no idea of the significant and lifelong impact I was making on my daughters until filming began. Prior to that (and after my conversion), I always felt I had room to grow as a husband, but I thought I had the dad thing down pretty well.

I had no clue.

As I interviewed more than eighty people for this film, God taught me something essential and life-changing in every interview about my dual roles as husband and father. There was so much I could be doing differently that would result in my family experiencing more blessings because of my obedience to a higher calling as a man. I just had to listen and apply.

A DAUGHTER NEEDS A FATHER'S ATTENTION

You've heard it said before, but it bears repeating: Time is your most valuable resource. Consider the fact that you'll likely have only eighteen years to truly parent your daughter. If you live to be eighty, only 22 percent of your time on earth will be devoted to her most defining years. Whatever you choose to do *instead* of being a dad while your daughter is still living in your house will eat into that time faster than you think. If we want to raise strong, courageous, godly women who'll be able to handle themselves once they're out of the house, we *must* give them our undivided attention.

Dr. Meg Meeker is one of the pivotal experts on the father-daughter relationship in my documentary. That shouldn't come as a surprise, given that she wrote *Strong Fathers, Strong Daughters*, a book that any father with a daughter should immediately buy. Her words cover this chapter because they're so insightful, and they were personally so meaningfully transformative in my relationship with my girls.

Dr. Meeker says, "Girls bond through talking and through listening, and so how dads speak is very important to daughters because we become intimate with people by talking . . . They need your time. They need your feelings. They need to hear you talk about anything. What are your opinions about things? What do you think about the president? What do you think about God? They need to see who you are as a person, and the only way you can do that is through spending time with them."

When I heard Dr. Meeker share that, I realized how deficient I'd been in sharing more about my life and opinions with my daughters. I'd done well at investing in my daughters' interests, but I'd allowed the shame of my past to discolor my perception of what my daughters would want to know about me. In the same way that I'd isolated myself from most everyone, I'd walled off certain experiences and topics from my daughters because I thought they either would not be interested or would think less of me as a father.

I had yet to realize my true stature in my daughters' eyes. As Dr. Meeker puts it, "Dads have no clue about the power that they have in their kids' lives. That's what dads need to understand: You may feel like a loser. You may feel like you're not earning enough money. You may not feel strong enough, smart enough, athletic enough. Your kids aren't thinking about that—particularly your daughters. They could care less. To them, you're enormous in their eyes."

A DAUGHTER NEEDS A FATHER'S AFFIRMATION

Before my life changed, I compared myself to my father and to the other men I knew who'd left their families. It was easy for me to believe that I was fulfilling my role as a dad because I didn't bail on my family when life got tough.

But this is the tragically low bar we've set for ourselves as fathers and husbands—just being there. That's not enough. We can't just "do our time" for eighteen years and hope for the best. We must be active in our daughters' lives, and that means being vocal, especially with words of affirmation. With girls, a dad's silence can be just as destructive or damaging as a father who talks to his daughters with demeaning or abusive language.

One of the most important things I've learned about raising girls is to let them know just how special they are to me as a father. Every day, I try to say something positive about each one of my girls: "Your hair looks cute," or "You did a great job on that test," or, simply, "I love you and I'm proud of you."

I try to compliment them not only on their physical beauty but also on their inner beauty. I'll say, "You are incredibly beautiful inside and out," and "You are amazing." I also try to call out the great things about each one them, and all three of my girls are different and unique in their own ways. The point is: Little girls must know, hear, and experience that their dads love them.

If a dad doesn't let his daughter know that she's cherished, she will search for that acceptance, affirmation, and attention from *any* other man, something no dad would purposely hope for his daughter.

Dr. Meeker speaks to why fathers should admire, compliment, and simply hang out with their daughters more often: "When she is in your company, your daughter tries harder to excel. When you teach her, she learns more quickly. When you guide her, she gains confidence. Boyfriends, brothers, even husbands can't shape her character the way you do. You will influence her entire life because she gives you an authority she gives no other man."

That place of authority isn't granted to you by default. You have to earn it through the attention, affirmation, and affection you lavish upon her. John Eldredge says,

> You get a little girl that's broken—doesn't know she's loved, doesn't know that she's beautiful and that she will be chosen—she will give herself in order to try and get that father love, try and get that assurance that she didn't get growing up. You get a dad who's blessing his daughter, she's going to know what kind of man to look for. She's going to know what to hold out for in a man. She's not going to settle for some

broken poser. She's going to wait for a good man who's going to love her well.

If a father steps into his role as a girl's role model for how a man should be, his words of affirmation can stem the tide of early sexual activity and teenage pregnancy. Dr. Meg Meeker reports,

They have found that girls who have an involved dad—he can even be divorced; he can be a single dad—but if Dad is involved and engaged with his daughters all through life, but particularly during the teen years, girls are less likely to be sexually active and hence become pregnant. And Dad is one of the biggest safety valves that a girl has as far as staying away from sexual activity. And again, she has her male needs met. She gets affection from her dad...

Girls who have engaged fathers feel better about themselves. They feel they're standing on solid ground. They're getting male affection and attention. And when their dad communicates to them, "No, this [sex] isn't something you should be doing. I believe that you can get through your teen years and through your college years, even wait until you're married. I believe that you should stay away from sexual activity until that time. I'm here to help you do that."

Even if Dad only says that once in his life, he has increased that girl's chances of not becoming sexually active exponentially. We moms can tell our daughters, but when Dad tells his daughter he believes that she should stay away from sex and she needs to stay away from sex, it's almost a done deal in her mind. It's the power of a dad.

Though Dr. Meeker's words felt like a heavy burden, it was one I would gladly bear for the benefit of my daughters. I didn't want them to learn how a man ought to treat them from some boy at school or some guy on TV. I wanted them to see it modeled in me so they could someday find a loving, caring, respectful, and godly man in due time.

A DAUGHTER NEEDS A FATHER'S AFFECTION

More than attention and affirmation, a daughter desperately desires a father's affection. They won't say this, and as they get older they may even deny this, but the truth remains: A daughter needs to feel that she's deeply and wholly loved by her father. Affection means hugging and the other appropriate measures of physical touch (which change as a daughter ages), but such affection is encompassed by a daughter's chief need from her father: to feel loved.

A daughter needs a father's love to show her how to be cherished and respected by a man. She longs for a man to be her father figure, mentor, and coach. If she doesn't receive a father's affection, she will go looking for it elsewhere. She will look to the world outside of her home for the love she's not hearing, receiving, and experiencing there. If she doesn't find affection at school or in another sphere of her life, she may turn to the last place any father would want his daughter to find examples of what a man should be: pop culture, which may make her feel good about herself for a time, but can never offer her the affection she actually wants and needs.

Dr. Meg Meeker spoke about the deep and abiding value of a father's affection for his daughter:

> There really is a dad hole in every daughter's heart. If a daughter doesn't have that hole filled with her dad, she will look anywhere to get it filled.
>
> One of the most common things that I see is adolescent girls turning to boys for attention, for love, for affection, even just to be touched. Girls will do anything just to be touched and to feel loved by a boy, and they'll have sex with any boy. Even though they may not like it, they will do it, because for that moment they feel that a man loves them.
>
> They'll play mind games with themselves, but then they leave that experience, it's very unfulfilling, and they feel lost, they feel empty still, and they go, "Well, since I have that feeling, something must be wrong with me. I'll try it again." So they go out and they try again with another boy, again with another boy.
>
> A dad's love is so fundamental to a girl's emotional, psychological, intellectual, mental health that if she doesn't have it, her intellectual, mental, psychological, emotional health is very fractured. It just is coming apart, and she really can't get her bearings. And she can't study. She can't function well.
>
> It's very interesting. We're finding now that even girls who are the product, if you will, of sperm donors, who are raised by a single mom—literally didn't have a dad—are going now and trying to find

who that man was who donated sperm. You see, there's that tie, that bind that is so strong they will seek out a stranger to identify him as Dad. That's why I call it a primal need. It's a primal drive that all girls have. That's how much it throws them off if they don't have Dad.

In other words, as Dr. Meeker also said, "If a daughter knows that she has her dad's love, life makes sense. If she doesn't know she has her dad's love, life doesn't make sense."

Even though I nodded my head to Dr. Meeker's and John Eldredge's insights, my heart wasn't truly opened to the vast influence that my displays of affection had on my daughters until Dr. Meeker shared a story with me off-camera. I wished we had still been filming.

On more than one occasion, a sexually active thirteen- or fourteen-year-old girl visited Dr. Meeker's office for a physical. The girl would check out fine, but before leaving she'd request a prescription.

Perplexed, Dr. Meeker would respond, "You're fine. Everything's good. You don't need a prescription."

Eyes downcast, the girl would reply, "I don't care what the prescription is for. Just put on the bottom of it 'Cannot have sex.'"

When Dr. Meeker first told me this story, I was confused. Why would a sexually active girl want a prescription that prevented her from having sex?

Dr. Meeker revealed the brutal truth: "You see, John, these girls were having sex, and it wasn't physically or emotionally pleasurable, but it was the only positive affection they were getting. They weren't getting any positive affection or love at home from their dads. This prescription was the girls' 'permission slip' they could give to their boyfriends to tell them, 'I can't have sex anymore.'"

I couldn't believe what I was hearing, but Dr. Meeker had firsthand experience of such occurrences on multiple occasions. I knew that a lack of affection could cause distance in a father-daughter relationship, but I didn't know it could cause such confusion and pain for a young girl.

Some men may read these words and feel a crushing weight of responsibility. They should. Fathers who desire to be good dads bear the heavy burden of modeling godly manhood to their daughters. It's a responsibility that can't be shirked without dire and likely lifelong consequences for the daughter.

Consider this: If the boys your teenage daughter chooses to date aren't up to your standards, what standards have you been modeling?

The man your daughter will marry is greatly influenced by the one she sees in you. If you doubt this truth, consider Dr. Meeker's take: "The reason women tend to marry somebody with very similar characteristics with their father is because they get so used to relating to a man they love in a certain way, and they don't know another way to do it, and it's subconscious. So, they just fold themselves back into that type of relationship because it's familiar. It's so deeply rooted in them. And that's why many girls who have been abused as youngsters by their dads end up marrying abusers, because that's all they know."

I interviewed a number of women for *The Father Effect* who all had absent fathers in one way or another. Their stories had a common thread of precisely what Dr. Meeker mentions: They were eventually attracted to men who were like their fathers.

Susan said, "I kind of went toward a father figure. I was looking for a dad. A dad that would pay attention to me…I chose someone just like my dad." In other words, she wanted someone who would pay attention to her, who would lavish love and affection on her, but she wound up finding someone like her dad: distant and detached.

Michelle spoke about how she felt the need to change who she was so that any man would love her: "I think you don't trust them [men], and so it goes back to you trying to do everything you think you should do to keep them. Not being yourself even. Becoming someone else, to keep them, so you don't lose that love."

Her experience echoes what Dr. Meeker described: "Something must be wrong with me." Because Michelle's father hadn't built the firm foundation of affection into her life, she sought it elsewhere, but to find it she believed she had to be anyone other than herself—because that obviously hadn't been enough for her father to love.

This is a tragic indictment of fathers. If we're not daily providing the affection our daughters need, we are failing them. By our indifference and reluctance to display affection, we are effectively telling them that who they are doesn't matter. Our lack of action speaks much louder than words and does not show our daughters how important they truly are to us. This has to stop. We can and must do better.

Girls who fail to receive a father's love will seek to fill, numb, or deny that need in any way, and the ramifications of their actions will likely reverberate throughout their lives.

DADDY'S LITTLE GIRLS LOVED

I often worry about my daughters' futures. I wonder what kind of legacy I'm leaving them. Since learning about the impact I have on their lives, I've striven to lavish attention, affirmation, and affection upon them—three of the most demanding sacrifices for a father to make.

We feel like we don't have time (*There's too much work to do or money to be made!*); or that we don't know the right words (*My dad never "affirmed" me, so I don't know how*); or that affection just isn't what we do (*Your mom can give you a hug*). But for as uncomfortable as some of these actions may make us feel, they are integral to our daughters' present and future well-being.

Men are often afraid to lavish attention, speak affirmation, and show affection to their daughters, but Dr. Meeker's solution is easy, and begins with the man who's responsible for his daughter's understanding of what a man should be: "The number one way to boost a girl's self-esteem isn't by... getting her on an elite soccer team, helping her get her grades up, or getting her to become a good dancer. It is... giving her physical affection from her dad. That's the number one way to boost a girl's self-esteem."

Dads, pay attention to your girls, tell them what they're worth in your eyes, and hug them every day. Be the kind of man you hope they marry someday. You won't always get it right, but they'll know that you're trying. If you do not lead your child in a positive direction, I guarantee the world will lead her in a negative one. But so long as she knows to the core of her being that you love her and will always do so, her self-worth will refuse to be lessened by anything this world may throw at her.

So how can you learn to better love your daughters?

By learning that *love* carries a multitude of meanings.

CHAPTER 15

WHAT IS LOVE?

A Direct Word to Fathers

"Your legacy is defined by the way you lead, love, and live every day. Lead boldly, love deeply, and live courageously."

Fathers, I'm going to let you in on a secret: Expressing your love for your children isn't hard. But it will demand two things from you that most of us are hesitant to give up: time and control. And just because you may not have received any evidence of love from your father doesn't get you off the hook for showing love to your children. In these pages, I hope to give you practical, actionable advice that can be easily implemented in your home, as long as you're willing to give up some time and control.

When Cathie shared the following story in my documentary, her words opened my eyes to how essential it was that I understand what love really is:

If I had a choice between a father verbally telling me he loved me, and the other choice would be actions, I would choose the action over the words. You can tell me all day long that you love me, and I hear that, and it goes into my spirit, but until you show me something, until you're there for me, or until you come home and take me to lunch, until you make me the most important thing in your life for a moment, you can tell me you love me forever, but it confuses me. What does that mean love is? Is telling me you love me—is that love?

I ran with "I love yous" for the rest of my life. And you can have people everywhere tell you they love you, and buy into the words, and then them not back it up with action. So it tends to re-create that same level of pain again and again and again. Because you don't have the experience to say, "Well, I really am glad that you love me, and I believe that you do, but could you show me?" You don't get there. You don't know that that's part of the process.

That's what love is. Love is being there.

If "love is being there," what does "being there" really mean?

LOVE IS TIME

What your children want from you more than anything else is your presence, not your presents. There is no substitute for time with your kids. It's what they will remember most. They'd rather you invest your time in them than your money.

Tom Lane said,

155

I think fathers make a mistake when they assume that things will be a good substitute for themselves. So when a dad says, "I know, I'm working extra hard. But I'm trying to provide good things for you and the kids," I don't know of a kid that would say, "Dad, please work harder. Don't come to the ball games. Don't spend any time with me. But make lots of money so that I can have everything that I want." If it comes right down to it, they'd rather have you than they would all the stuff. They'd rather have you at their ball game. They'd rather have you eat dinner with them. They'd rather have you put them to bed at night.

Waylon Ward echoed those thoughts, and his words made me think back to all the times my dad failed to make time for me because he was "working":

I think the biggest mistake could be summarized around thinking that what I provide for my kids is more important than being with my kids. Providing for them is [important]; that's one evidence of love, but it gives them the wrong idea about what love is. Spending time with them and being emotionally connected with them is so much more significant than providing for them. A kid that's fourteen is not going to care in twenty years how much money you had in the bank when he was fourteen. But he'll remember you playing catch with him. He'll remember you being at the ball game with him.

A child can't assume your love. They must see, hear, and feel your love on a daily basis. They must know beyond a shadow of a doubt that their father loves them for no other reason than being their child. Such love is demonstrated more than spoken, and it costs more than anything you could ever buy for your child. What a man does and what he shows trumps what he says. If faith without action isn't faith (see James 2:14), love without action isn't love.

You can't tell your son, "Good job, champ," if you've missed his ball game. You can't tell your daughter, "You danced so well," if you missed her recital. The words ring hollow within their ears because you failed to show your love by simply choosing to be with them over anyone and anything else. To feel loved is to feel prized and prioritized. And that means making time for your children, even when it's inconvenient.

Pastor Dudley Hall shared, "A kid knows how important he is by how much time and how much sacrifice you're willing to make to get involved." You don't have to be perfect. You just need to be present.

According to Dr. Meeker, when a father purposefully spends time with his children,

> what happens in that child's self-esteem is huge. This figure who's larger-than-life in my eyes wants my company. If he wants my company, there must be something good about me. There must be something he enjoys about me. He sees me. He likes what he sees. He's a really smart guy and he wants to have a conversation with me. I must be smart. I must be fun.
>
> That's why time is so important, because those are the messages that kids get when they spend time with Dad. They just want to know that you want to be with

them. The best thing a dad can do is to engage his kids. That when you're with your kids, listen to your kids, look at them when you're talking to them, be courteous to them, express your feelings to them. I think, just be who you are to your kids because…all your kids really want is Dad. They just want Dad.

For all my years of drunken wandering and barely holding on to my family, I'd actually thought that I was doing a pretty good job of raising my girls—because I was providing well for them. What I didn't understand then was that providing a house and material goods for them wasn't at all what they needed or desired. They needed a father who could provide time, and I was a man who was perfectly content to waste mine on business trips with people I barely knew.

I shake my fist at the father I used to be, knowing that I can never recover or relive those years. But because of Dr. Meeker's excellent books and what I learned through making *The Father Effect* documentary, I know better now. By no means am I a perfect father, but I consciously make time for each of my daughters. Now I trust God to provide for our family, and I worry more about the impact I'm having on my daughters.

Fatherhood is a gift like no other. Cherish every moment.

LOVE IS UNCONDITIONAL

Unfortunately, the natural inclination of men comes into play in all of our relationships. Because we're driven to compete, we're driven by performance. We want to "do" (whatever we want) more than we want to speak or feel. It's why our minds immediately jump to solutions when our wives share their challenges with us. While our problem-solving techniques are useful in some settings—business and sports, our stereotypical escapes from domesticity—they're antithetical to raising a family. To love through performance is to love conditionally, and to love conditionally really isn't to love at all.

The love you show your kids should not be based on their performance. I've witnessed the tragedy of performance-based parenting at far too many of my kids' sporting events. I've seen a dad blatantly ignore his son after a game because the son played poorly, as if the son's supposed lack of effort were an indictment of the father. Your kids need to know you love them because of who they are, not who you want them to be. Consequently, I've worked hard to ensure that I hug or kiss my girls after their games regardless of how they've played. I desperately want them to know that I love them because they're my daughters and not for what they can accomplish.

Plus, if you choose to show love based on performance, your kids just might measure their love for you based on your fluctuating love for them, or on your perceived performance as a parent. Your love has to be all-in, no-holds-barred, and consistent. Your children need to know you are proud of them, believe in them, and love them no matter what mistakes they make.

You may not like what they do sometimes, and they may aggravate you beyond exasperation, but your love should never waver from "You are my child, and because of that you are loved." Your children need to know there is nothing they can do to make you love them any more or any less. God's love is not performance-based, and ours should not be either.

The children of the fatherless who become parents might have trouble with this because it wasn't modeled for us. Many of us likely felt conditionally loved for most of our lives, and it's hard to be freed from that kind of model. If our eyes and hearts haven't been opened to what unconditional love actually looks and sounds like, we're blind and deaf to it. We haven't experienced it, so we don't know how to give it.

Which is why it's all the more important for the children of the fatherless to fully surrender their lives to God. The catch-22 of our situation is that no human can ever truly love another person unconditionally. We're all prone to performance-based love because of our natural sinful tendencies toward selfishness and pride. Men are particularly this way because we're competitive and we like to know whether we're measuring up—and whether others are measuring up to us.

The only true form of unconditional love comes from God, and until you've experienced that kind of incredible love washing over you, you may not have an inkling of how to show such love to others. Therefore, I implore you to seek God. Even if you don't know what to say, the simple choice to reach out to Him will be enough. Through experiencing His kind of love, you'll begin to understand how to love your children less conditionally than before.

LOVE IS VULNERABILITY

It's easy to be a dad when life is good, but defining moments come when life is difficult, and those are the ones your kids will remember most.

For instance, as I wrote this book, a family conversation took a dive into theologically deep waters. My oldest daughter was struggling with life in general. She'd been asking herself the big questions: *Why do bad things happen to good people? If God's so strong, why doesn't He do something to stop suffering?* She became distraught.

As I vainly tried to answer her questions—to fix her present problem—I became emotional, too. Whatever rational answers I gave her just didn't seem to work. Finally, I told her about my struggles with depression. I began to weep. I cried because I didn't want my daughter to hurt. I cried because I couldn't provide adequate answers. And I cried because I've always been afraid that my depressive tendencies would be passed down to my daughters. I couldn't bear the thought of any of them having to carry such a burden.

After sharing more about my life, I asked my family to stand and pray with me. Holding onto one another, we prayed for my oldest daughter. We group-hugged as we asked God for help to see us through this difficult time and the ones we would face in the future. I'd like to believe that even as hard as that conversation was, no one in my family—and particularly my eldest daughter—will ever forget it.

We are not perfect, and our kids need to know that so they understand they don't have to be perfect either. But to get to that point, I had to get over myself. I had to place my fears in God's hands and effectively show my cards to my daughters.

I had to get vulnerable, and that's a hard place for a man to get to. If you wrestle with vulnerability, you will inevitably be presented with an unmistakable situation in which to reveal your heart to your child. But it won't be easy.

I believe a man can best show his vulnerability through apologizing for his wrongheaded words and actions. I'll let Dr. Meeker cover the power of a father's apologies:

When a dad asks for forgiveness and apologizes to a child, it draws that child very, very close to Dad. That child now feels that he or she can trust Dad more. Dad's smart. Dad is strong because Dad acknowledges his mistakes. But now Dad's going to do something about it. He said shut up or he swore at me, and now he said that was wrong. "I apologize. I'm not going to do that again." That makes me feel so good. My dad is so great. Now I can really trust my dad to do the right thing because it didn't feel right to me, it didn't feel good. He's going to make it right.

You see, now that child feels so close to Dad. Isn't that what we all want with our kids? We want to be closer with our kids. Now that child is going to trust Dad a whole lot more. Would you as a dad want to miss out on all that? That's what you miss out on when you are too proud to go to your child and say, "I am so sorry I said what I said. I'm so sorry that I did what I did. Will you forgive me?"

Men are usually terrible at apologies. Maybe that's why we try to buy off our loved ones, just so we don't have to say those dreaded words: I'm sorry. We hope and assume that our wives understand that chocolate plus flowers equals regret. And maybe that's why, when a man verbalizes his apology—and he doesn't just say sorry, but he's very specific about what he's apologizing for—a man's vulnerability in front of those he loves is so powerful and transformative.

Just imagine if your dad apologized to you right now and took the blame for everything you've ever laid at his feet.

You'd consider him differently, wouldn't you?

LOVE IS AFFECTION

Most men struggle to show affection to the ones they love. In our relationships with our wives, most of us want to skip the bases and head to home as soon as possible. Either we're uncomfortable with affection or we wrongly assume that physical touch ought to always lead to the bedroom.

That discomfort with affection affects our children as well. When we struggle to hug our sons or daughters, we cause them to seek that affection elsewhere. This consequence is particularly pronounced in daughters, where the failure of a father to show appropriate affection can often result in that daughter seeking affection from *any* other man who shows the least bit of affection for her. Fathers, your first line of defense against every man who will enter your daughter's life is your displays of affection for her. When she feels protected and loved by you, she won't need to search for it elsewhere.

I take great pride in the fact that my fifteen- and seventeen-year-old daughters still hold my hand as we walk to dinner on a date night and that they'll sit in my lap at home or at someone else's house as we visit. They're not ashamed of the love I have for them.

Fathers who show affection for their sons may be an even rarer breed. But Neal Jeffrey described what all men need: "I think every man longs to be loved and hugged by their father. Every boy wants that. Of course, there are a huge number of men who never had a dad who hugged them, too; who told them, 'Hey son, I love you, and I'm proud of you,' and they long for that." Even the briefest of hugs given on a consistent basis allows a son to know and feel his father's strong love for him.

LOVE IS SPOKEN

I know, I know. I began this section by saying that actions matter more than words when it comes to showing love for your children. But that doesn't mean you can just show up to every ball game or recital and *never* say, "I love you." Those three words carry immense weight when spoken from a father's mouth to his child's ears.

David Vestal, a pastor and former Dallas police detective, is right: "One of the biggest mistakes I think we make with our kids is just assuming that they know we love them, assuming that they know we care, instead of reaching out to them and saying, 'I want you to know I love you. I am really proud of the woman of God that you are, the man of God that you are. I want you to know that I am never too busy for you.'"

We must say the words we hope our actions convey.

Dr. Meeker said:

It's very important that dads verbalize to their kids, "I love you. You're great. You're patient. You're capable." It sounds pretty basic. A lot of dads say, "Why do I have to do that? My kids know that." But your kids don't really know that.

You need to tell your kids "I love you" because kids don't think about the fact that Dad has provided them with this home or Dad has given them a good education...All they know is how they feel, and they need to know every day.

In order to be successful at school...they need to know they're standing on solid ground. The ground is only solid if they know when they walk out the door in the morning and go to school that Dad loves them and believes in them—then life is good.

The best way to affirm your child depends on their specific needs. Daughters usually want to know they're loved. They want to hear that they're beautiful both inside and out. Boys often want to know that they're capable. They want to hear that they have what it takes and that they're doing a great job.

In particular, boys need to hear verbal affirmation from their fathers that they're growing into men. Pastor Dudley Hall describes that necessity so well: "No boy ever knows he's a man until a father tells him. A woman can't tell you. I mean, she can tell you, but it won't make sense to you. And until a father looks you in the eye and says, 'I declare you a man,' you will be always trying to find that affirmation."

Your kids will always have their share of critics, but you should not be one of them. Even if you might be joking with

165

them or using sarcasm, either they won't know your intended effect, or your words will still sting despite their casual nature. Either way, you're no longer building up your child. They'll hear the negativity more than anything else.

Consequently, refrain from saying anything that could be perceived as tearing down your child. By all means, be a parent and course-correct when necessary, but do so in a way that's always undergirded by "You can trust me because I love you."

The words you speak to your children today will echo in the hearts of the generations that follow them. Every day, speak words of life and love.

LOVE IS FROM GOD

Your kids are following you. It's your choice where you lead them.

When I think about the immensity of this challenge, I'm reminded of Proverbs 22:6: "Start children off on the way they should go, and even when they are old they will not turn from it." Of course, that makes parenting seem like an even more monumental task—now I'm on the hook for my children's children!—but God uses that verse to remind me of the sober responsibility I have as a steward of His creations.

It's your responsibility to help your child be who God wants them to be, not who you want them to be. He knew who He wanted them to be long before you were ever born. The chief way you can ensure that they long to follow God is to do what this chapter has said all along: Model the behavior you want to see revealed in your child.

I love how David Vestal put it when I asked him, "What do you think is the best thing a father can do for his children?" He said, "Be a man of God honestly. You can get into the accolades of encouraging your kids and things of that nature, but I want to be the man that God's called me to be in front of my son. When I am that man, I walk in a strength and in a presence that I could never accomplish on my own."

When you choose to relinquish your death grip on your ego and offer to give up your ideas of success for God's definition of success in the home, God will provide you with the time, patience, and love you'll need to see it through.

And the chief reason you may need to reassess your relationship with God? Dr. Meeker answers, "The reason it's important for dads to teach their kids about God is because you are your kids' first reflection of male love. You put a template over their hearts for how they're going to relate to all male figures—including God. You are the conduit to God, the first male conduit to God."

Now, when I think about *that* kind of burden, I can barely comprehend it—which is why I'm so grateful that the burden isn't mine alone to bear. When I fear that I'm not measuring up, when I'm not modeling the kind of dad I think my girls should have, when my life doesn't look like the kind of godly life I desire to lead, I think about 1 Peter 5:6–7: "Humble yourselves, therefore, under God's mighty hand, that he may lift you up in due time. Cast all your anxiety on him because he cares for you." Knowing that my Father loves me helps me know that I can be a father who loves his children well, too.

To love your child, give them your time.

Love them without condition, just as God loves you.

Humble yourself and show your vulnerability.

Don't be afraid to show affection.

Speak words of love constantly.

And let God's love always be your example.

To incorporate these lofty ideas into your daily routine, just turn the page.

CHAPTER 16

FATHERLY ADVICE

Practical Steps Toward Becoming a Better Father

"Every day is a new opportunity to be a better father."

When I'm old and gray and sitting on my porch in a rocking chair next to my wife, I want to be able to think of my daughters and *know* that I did the best I could to be the man they needed me to bc. These are the steps I've taken, or have heard of other men taking, to become the kind of father I always wanted to have.

SPEAK LOVE; SHOW LOVE

The fundamental need of every child is to know that their dad loves them, is proud of them, and believes in them. Your kids long for your approval. If you're not telling them you love them *and* showing it, they won't believe they're wanted, loved, or cherished.

If words of affirmation don't come quickly or easily to your lips, start simple: Make it a point to tell your child, every day, "I love you," and "I'm proud of you." Look into their eyes as you say it. Don't say it casually. Say it intentionally so they can't doubt what you mean.

Remember, they need to hear those words from you, but they also need to see your actions match. If you're not around when they need you—and that can mean your physical presence as well as your attention and emotional availability—they will feel the disconnect between your words and your actions. You must reveal that your words are true by displaying love to them. To a child, showing love can equal one of two things: spending time with them and showing affection.

IMPACT YOUR KIDS DAILY

To help me become a more consistent verbal encourager of my kids, I devised an acronym for the word *impact*. I knew that if I wanted to be the kind of father I wished I had, I needed to be intentional in raising my kids. I needed to walk in daily awareness of my impact. Now, when I think of *impact*, I think: Identify Moments of Positive Affirmation in your Child Today. Then I follow that command.

MAKE YOUR FAMILY PROUD OF YOUR FAMILY

A 2013 study on African American and Latino male gang members in Los Angeles County cited "frustration and anxiety stemming from family problems such as fatherlessness" as a chief motivation for joining a gang. The study also reported that "only 1 out of the 8 members in this study had a father that lived at home."[9] In other words, what gang members lack in acceptance and affirmation from their fathers, they find within the confines of a gang. I think that's why gang members become so attached and so proud of their gang association.

Of course, I'm not advocating for turning your family into a violent gang, but I am saying that you want to instill the same kind of sense of belonging in each of your children when they think about your family. You want them to be proud of who they are and to whom they're related.

An easy way to do this is to talk about your family as a unit. For instance, everyone in my family will often talk about "the Finches" doing this or that. In other words, it's not just the single person who accomplishes something; rather, it's the family gang.

CREATE UNIQUE TRADITIONS

Another way to encourage family unity that also involves spending focused, quality time with your children is to create family traditions. They don't have to be elaborate or even serious. For instance, more impromptu John Finch rap songs have greeted my girls at birthday parties, holidays, and any chance I get to show my mad rap skillz than they'd likely ever have wanted, but that's a silly way I consistently show them my care. Because it's happened so often, it's a tradition. On certain occasions, they nearly expect a rap now!

On a more serious note, traditions can be used to heal a family. After suffering the loss of his wife and the mother of his three young daughters, a friend of mine named Guy incorporated family cook nights. To ensure that he maintained close connections to his daughters during an emotionally tumultuous time in their family's life, he mandated that all four of them prepare a meal once a week, together. I respect Guy for that kind of faithful parenting. Where most men might have withdrawn from everyone or sought solace in any number of temptations, Guy chose to be a father when his girls needed him the most. I'd like to think that simple ritual of just cooking one meal a week together helped them all heal.

DON'T DISMISS THE SMALL THINGS

It takes only a moment to make a memory your kids will never forget. Have a special "thing" that you do with each of your children. It could be as simple as a secret handshake that you never share with anyone else in the house. It could be a special place that you take them for a treat. (My oldest daughter loves Bahama Buck's, a shaved-ice franchise.)

It could be, and I probably shouldn't put this in print, getting over yourself and surrendering to your child's outlandish whims—like getting a mani-pedi with your daughter where she picks out Dad's hot-pink nail polish color, or letting your daughter give you a complete makeover with lipstick, blush, a wig, and far too much mascara.

Not that I would know from experience.

These aren't difficult things to begin doing with each of your children, and they will show how special you think each of your children are because you have a special "thing" with them.

KISS YOUR KIDS TWICE A DAY

To show my affection for them, I try to kiss my daughters in the morning and at night. I also use that as an opportunity to verbally encourage them by saying things like "Good morning, sunshine," "I'm praying for you today," or "What can I do to help you get ready for the day?" These sentences aren't even that long, but I'd like to assume hearing them makes a world of difference in how their days begin.

I'll kiss them again right before they go to bed, and I'll reiterate that I love them, that I'm proud of them, and that I believe in them. Some nights I'll go a step further and point out something positive they accomplished that day. I want them to go to bed safe and secure in their father's love. I want them to see, hear, and feel how cherished they are in my eyes.

MODEL MANLINESS

Of course, I mean *manliness* in its simplest form: Show your children what it truly means to be a man, which has nothing to do with external strength or what the culture says men ought to be. As their father, you're modeling the standard that men in your daughter's life ought to live up to and by which your son will measure himself as a man, husband, and father. Set it high.

One of the best and easiest ways to do this is to hug and show love to your wife in front of your kids every chance you get. Speak words of affirmation to her in front of them. Realize that you're modeling either how you want your son to treat his future wife or how your daughter ought to expect to be treated by her future husband.

Your kids will view their relationship with God through the filter of their relationship with you. How you interact with them can significantly affect how they might interact with God.

Real men rise to these kinds of challenges.

PRAY FOR YOUR CHILDREN

In *The Father Effect*, former pro quarterback Neal Jeffrey says, "There is nothing like a child hearing his father pray for him out loud by name in that manly, fatherly voice."

During his playing days, Neal's father would grab him and pray with him before and after every football game—even as Neal became an adult. When his dad couldn't make it to an NFL game in a faraway city, Neal's dad would write him a note of encouragement. To hear Neal talk about his father is to hear a son who was deeply affected by his father's consistent prayer for his son.

Whether it's in the morning, at night, or both, make it

a point to pray with your child every day. When they're old enough to understand you, ask your child what they'd like for you to pray about on their behalf. Then pray out loud, and be sure to speak their names. That's the kind of spiritual modeling that I think is lacking in far too many of our homes today.

Be sure to pray for your wife in front of her and your children, too. Offer words of thanksgiving and blessing that your family has been given such an amazing mom and wife. Make sure your family knows that you pray for each of them by name.

If you've never done this or have been inconsistent about it in the past, don't worry about the awkwardness you or your child might feel when you initiate daily prayers. As long as you're consistent and earnest, that time of day will become your new normal and even expected. The hope is that modeling prayer for your children will open their minds and hearts to God's leading and that they'll learn they can pray at any time for any reason—even when you're not there.

Plus, it may just start a consistency in prayer in your own life.

I ask my ten-year-old to pray for us once a week. It's the highlight of my day when she does. I love to hear the words of an innocent child talking to God. Listening to her pray for us amazes me. Nothing matches it. What's fascinating, but shouldn't be surprising given that I now know how much parents model for their kids, is that she'll often use some of the same phrases I've used when praying for her out loud. That's priceless, and it reminds me that my kids are always listening.

SPEND UNINTERRUPTED TIME WITH YOUR CHILDREN

Spending time with your child isn't the same as spending intentional, quality time with them. Put your phone in a different room. Unplug your laptop. Turn off the TV. Devote *at least* fifteen minutes of your day to each of your children. If you have more than one child, they *each* get at least fifteen minutes. Give them your undivided attention.

Don't do all the talking either. Allow your child to speak, and listen to what they're saying. Your kids need to know that you're interested and invested in what they're telling you. They will know and feel that only if you're making eye contact and actually listening to what they're saying.

I love what counselor Dwayne Collins said about listening:

The overall thing is to listen to the child. That doesn't mean you come in and you say, "Okay, how was your day?" and you listen for two or three minutes while they try to talk to you. It means being there and listening, and sometimes it means getting down on the floor so that you're not looking down at the child, but you're down there on his level...

I think a lot of the things that are wrong in marriages and in families is that we don't know because we don't listen, and our tendency is that when our wives or our kids try to talk to us, we're planning our response instead of listening to what they say.

The next time your child wants to talk, work at becoming a better listener. Get on their level. Invest in their interests. Try to stop responses from building in your mind as they talk. Place yourself in their tiny shoes and try to remember what it was like when you were their age. Recall the hope of spending just a few uninterrupted moments with Dad and the frustration of knowing that he was present but not listening. Engage your child in conversation, but let him or her lead the way.

TAKE YOUR CHILD OUT

One of the most incredibly effective means of giving your undivided attention to your child is to set aside a night, maybe once a month, where it's just you and that child. Let them pick what they want to do (within reason!), but make sure some time is built in where the two of you can just talk. If you've never done this before, you'll be amazed at how your child may open up to you away from home and during this special time.

Daddy-daughter date nights give you the opportunity to show her how she should be treated by a man. They also provide a safe place for her to ask questions of you she may never have asked at home. And because of the closeness these kinds of dates build, you can ask questions you may not have asked at home simply because you have the time and space to do so now.

When thinking about what to talk about, seek to get to know your daughter beyond what you already know (or think you know). I like to ask, "What's your favorite class right now?" or "Who are your top three friends and why?" or "If you could be anyone in the world, who would you be?" These kinds of real-life and hypothetical questions may just reveal a whole new person to you. They also offer gateways to more serious discussions. And because kids can change so quickly, you can likely reuse the questions a few times.

For sons, scheduling a man's night allows for the same kind of closeness to develop. A son needs to see what his father enjoys outside of the home and his job, and it provides a father the opportunity to shape his son into a man. Going to a ball game provides ample time to talk about sports, which is often a great metaphor for just about anything else in life. And because it's just the two of you, he's likely to talk about things he's too embarrassed to talk about at home (the same goes for you, too).

If you haven't scheduled these kinds of outings with your child before, make a big deal about them. Circle them in red on your calendar. Mention it the week before it happens, then treat the night like an extra-special event where that child is your sole focus.

To imagine the kind of impact those nights could have, especially as they become an expected part of a child's routine, just think if you could have experienced such nights with your own father.

TELL THEM YOUR STORY

I don't know what prompted her to ask me, but one night as I was putting my girls to bed, my youngest asked, "Dad, what was your first job?"

I replied, "Well, you might not believe this, but I was a rat."

All of my girls laughed. "No, really, what was your first job?"

"I really was a rat! I worked at a pizza place called Chuck E. Cheese's, and their mascot was a big rat. So when I had that job, I had to dress up like a rat every day!"

They got the biggest kick out of that, and before I knew it, I'd spent two hours with them, telling them about every job I'd had as a teenager.

I believe every child, young and old, has an innate curiosity to know what their dad was like. Never discount your experience as something not worth sharing with your kids, even if some of those experiences don't paint you in the best light. Of course, you'll need to use discretion depending on your child's age, but hearing the stories of what you were like before they came along is fascinating. These kinds of stories help them to get to know you much more deeply, and they can also open up insightful conversations.

Also, even though it might be difficult, tell them about your father. What was he like when you were a child? How did he treat you? What did he do for a living? What did you like about him? What didn't you like? Hearing about your father will enable your children to understand his influence on your life. They won't be able to see how deeply you may have been affected, but they'll get an inkling of why Dad is the way he is.

ASK FOR FORGIVENESS

I wonder how many fathers ask forgiveness of their children—particularly of their young ones. It seems you often hear more about fathers with grown children asking forgiveness for the way they treated them when they were young. But you don't often hear about fathers apologizing to small children and teenagers.

When you mess up, ask your kids to forgive you. Not only does this show your vulnerability, but it also lets your kids know that you're human and prone to making mistakes. It models how responsible adults ought to act when they hurt someone else, whether intentionally or not. It reveals to them how God treats us, forgiving us when we don't deserve it.

Your children need to understand that you're not perfect; otherwise, they might believe they *have* to be perfect. When a father can't admit his wrongs, his children will believe the same about themselves: *I don't need to apologize for anything because I haven't done anything wrong.* Plus, if you project a perfect persona, your kids will be immensely let down when you do inevitably fail them. The perfect-hero dad you've tried so hard to be will become a disappointment.

The most specific example I can give, because I think it's the most common and I know I've been guilty of doing this on too many occasions, is losing your temper and yelling at your kids. When you do this, consider these steps:

1. Wait for you and your child's tempers to cool.
2. With full intention, ask for their forgiveness while looking your child in the eye.
3. Apologize directly to them.
4. Be specific in explaining why you yelled.
5. Hug them.

If you don't explain the reason for your behavior, your children will believe it's okay to lose their tempers and yell at others. But when you can admit fault and explain why you lashed out, they'll see a much better example of how to handle one's emotions, even after they've just witnessed how *not* to handle one's emotions. You always model what you want to see come to life in your children. Model humility.

SEEK COUNSELING

When I first decided to seek healing for my father wound, I knew I needed someone to help me. I'd done life so poorly on my own for so long that I knew I couldn't free myself from the prison I'd trapped myself within. The door that would release me had to be opened from the other side.

When I finally understood my need for outside help, I compared it to deep-sea fishing. For the best outcome to a deep-sea fishing expedition, hiring a guide is essential. An experienced guide reveals the best place to catch a blue marlin, provides the right kind of fishing pole and bait, and shows the proper technique to reel in a great catch. In other words, when it came to counseling, I needed someone to tell me everything I didn't know, which was as vast as the ocean.

Still, when I thought about seeing a therapist, my ego puffed up. *Everyone knows that anyone who sees a therapist is weak. Or he's a wacko. Or both. At the very least, people will know you have* major *problems.* The funny thing with my thinking was that I *did* have major problems! But society and Satan had convinced me that seeking help wasn't manly because it appeared to display weakness. I know better now: It takes a real man to admit his issues and take the necessary steps to find healing, regardless of the bruising his ego may suffer.

Check your ego at the door of your heart. Seek a biblical counselor who will help you better understand yourself, your history, your father, your family, and God. This is your only life, and the only time you have to make it right is right now.

SEEK GOD

Maybe it should go without saying in a book about fathers and children written from a Christian perspective that you ought to seek God, but those two simple words will give you the strength, encouragement, and hope to keep proceeding down a road of forgiveness that will most assuredly not be easy.

Your kids learn to make God a priority in their lives by watching you make Him a priority in yours. Are you? If not, consider this: God longs for you to admit your weaknesses so that He might be made strong within you (see 2 Cor. 12:9).

If you've wrestled through life and felt afflicted on every side because of the way your father failed to love, care, or provide for you, you already know that you can't do life on your own. If you're tired of being lonely, angry, confused, frustrated, or depressed, seek God. The pursuit of money and success could be one of the biggest regrets of your life. Don't lose focus on what really matters: God and family. Fully surrender to what God wants from your life and allow Him to do something tremendous with the rest of your days.

Of all the regrets I have, my biggest is failing to see what God was desperately trying to reveal to me for so many years. I was deaf to His voice and blind to His leading. I wanted nothing more than to be a man that women would want and men would want to be. I sought to be the life of the party because I didn't feel alive anywhere else. I drank to numb the daily pain. I isolated myself from my family and chose to spend more time with people I hardly even knew. I pushed God into the corners of my life until I left Him with no room at all in which to work.

Had I only looked up from my self-centeredness sooner, I would have realized that the father I'd longed to have for so long had been there for me the entire time. My Father God had never left me, would never abandon me, and would always be there for me. When I finally said, "You're enough for me, God," that's when my life changed irrevocably for the better.

EPILOGUE
LETTER TO MY FATHER

April 4, 2017

Dear Dad,

I wish you were here. I would love for you to meet my amazing wife and see just how blessed I am as a husband and father. I wish you were here to see my girls, your granddaughters, and the proud smile on your face as you see the incredible young women they are becoming. I would love to hear you laugh at the funny things they say and do.

I wish you were here to comfort Mom and love her like I saw you do so many times as you danced together in our living room. I wish I could hear you sing one more time as if you had not a care in the world. I wish you would have known how much I love you and miss you then and now. I wish you knew the man I am today, and I wish I could just sit with you and ask you all the questions I have wanted to ask you since you've been gone.

I wish you would have known it's okay to be broken, we all are, and that there is hope no matter what you are going through. I wish you had known that you were not alone and the only one going through the pain of what you were struggling with.

I wish you would have had a loving and caring father. And I wish you would have known about the father wound and sought help to find healing and freedom.

Most importantly, I wish you could know that I have forgiven you and I hope you have forgiven me for all the years I spent angry at you. I now understand why you did what you did. I cannot wait to one day see you again.

I miss you and I love you.

Your son,
John

Dear Dad,

I wish you were here. I would love for you to meet my amazing wife and see just how blessed I am as a husband and father. I wish you were here to see my girls, your granddaughters, and the proud smile on your face as you see the incredible young women they are becoming. I would love to hear you laugh at the funny things they say and do. I wish you were here to comfort mom and love her like I saw you do so many times as you danced together in our living room. I wish I could hear you sing one more time as if you had not a care in the world. I wish you would have known how much I love you and miss you then and now. I wish you knew the man I am today and I wish I could just sit with you and ask you all the questions I have wanted to ask you since you've been gone. I wish you would have known it's okay to be broken, we all are, and that there is hope no matter what you are going through. I wish you had known that you were not alone and the only one going through the pain of what you were struggling with. I wish you would have had a loving and caring father. And I wish you would have known about the father wound and sought help to find healing and freedom. Most importantly, I wish you could know that I have forgiven you and I hope you have forgiven me for all the years I spent angry at you. I now understand why you did what you did. I cannot wait to one day see you again. I miss you and I love you.

Your Son,
John

ACKNOWLEDGMENTS

I am incredibly thankful for Michelle, my wife: You support and inspire no matter how crazy my ideas are or how chaotic our life gets. The film, book, and the man I am today would not exist without your never-ending love and encouragement. You are truly more than I deserve.

I am incredibly thankful for my girls, Ellie, Brooke, and Sydney: You inspire me every day to be a better father and make me feel blessed, proud, and honored to be the man you call Dad.

I am blessed and thankful for my mom, Pattye: Your courage, faith, and love have forever influenced my life in ways you will never know. You truly are one in a million.

I am thankful for my brothers, Larry and Scott: You have supported me through the crazy journey of our lives together, and I will always be indebted to you for the great examples you set as my older brothers. Just remember: I have always been Mom's favorite and that's just something you will have to learn to live with.

I am thankful for my nephews, Cody Finch, Luke Finch,

ACKNOWLEDGMENTS

and Wes Finch: You continue to set the bar high for my girls in your example of what studly, godly, and amazing young men look like by the way you live your lives and love your wives and kids. You guys inspire me, and I dig your chili!

I am thankful for Sherilyn Finch, Erin Finch, Haley Finch, and Lauren Finch: You have made the Finch men in my life the loving and honorable men they are. We are truly blessed and grateful for you.

I am thankful for my father-in-law and mother-in-law, George and Marguerite Carpenter: I am very blessed and fortunate to have such amazing in-laws and for your steadfast love, support, and encouragement. (And I am very thankful for the perfect daughter you raised!)

I am thankful for all the people I interviewed for the film and book: You were patient enough to spend some time with me and share your honest, raw, and sometimes very emotional memories. The film and book are possible because of you and your willingness to share your stories.

I also want to thank John Eldredge, Dr. Meg Meeker, Gordon Dalbey, Neal Jeffrey, Dr. John Sowers, Dudley Hall, Larry Titus, Tom Lane, Brady Boyd, Tom Davis, Paul Cole, and the many others who are faithful in their calling to spread the word about the importance of fathers: Thank you so much for your dedication to change the lives of many in this generation and for generations to come.

I am thankful for a bunch of brothers named Ben Arment, Brian Hackney, Kirk Massey, Burney Roberts, Guy Delcambre, Mick Moffitt, David Werch, Rick Smith, Jason Ward, Jon Allen, John Wright, Darren Barton, Charles Robinson, John

ACKNOWLEDGMENTS

Adams, Keith Osborn, Rick Browning, David Bird, Steve Lineweaver, Jeff Cureton, David Vestal, Jeff Dotson, Brian Massey, Mike Belt, Scott Meador, Brian Goslee, Chris Peters, Terry Snarr, Paul O'Rear, Ray Asay, John Pugh, Darrel Rundus, Chris Roach, Christopher Shawn Shaw, Scott Sherwood, Tyler Wood (and many others I'm sure I forgot to include): You have continued to encourage me through the struggles of getting this message out and moving forward with the mission God has given me. God used you in times you probably don't even know about, and I am forever grateful for your faithfulness to Him!

I am thankful for my counselor, Dr. Tom Larussa: God used you to help me through the most difficult time in my life, and I can't thank you enough for your gift of advice and counsel. Thank you, Dr. Tom.

I am thankful for my literary agent, David Van Diest: I am grateful for your passion and belief in the project and story and for all your hard work in making this book possible. Thanks so much, brother!

I am thankful for Blake Atwood, my cowriter: You are an incredibly blessed and gifted writer who put up with my insanity and made sense of my madness and mountains of disconnected thoughts and writings. I still don't know how you did it. You are incredible, bro, and I greatly appreciate you!

I am thankful for my earthly father, James Henry Finch: You did the best with what you had, and you tried with all that you had to provide a good and loving home for your family. I love you, Dad, and I cannot wait to see you again.

Last, and most importantly, I am forever changed and

ACKNOWLEDGMENTS

thankful for God, my heavenly Father: Your life-changing power of forgiveness gave me not only a second chance to be the man, husband, and father You created me to be, but also the opportunity to share Your story of grace, redemption, and love.

Special thanks to Jon Paul for helping me get the rights back from my publisher and for all your support in getting books into prisons.

Thank you Percy Lee Kennedy Jr. for opening the doors for us to share God's message of hope and healing to those behind the walls.

190

NOTES

1 "Barack Obama Podcast: On Fatherhood," YouTube video, 4:40, posted by "BarackObama.com," June 17, 2007, https://www.youtube.com/watch?v=CURvgDRDg3M.

2 "Dennis Rodman Basketball Hall of Fame Induction Speech," YouTube video, 1:05, posted by "Prince Marketing Group," April 4, 2012, https://www.youtube.com/watch?v=tHu6pMjL1ew.

3 Walter Isaacson, *Steve Jobs*, read by Dylan Baker (New York: Simon & Schuster, 2011), audiobook; 25 hrs.

4 CBSNews.com staff, "The Delinquents: A Spate of Rhino Killings," *CBS News*, August 22, 2000, http://www.cbsnews.com/news/the-delinquents.

5 Gordon Dalbey, *Sons of the Father: Healing the Father-Wound in Men Today* (Folsom, CA: Civitas Press, 1992).

NOTES

6 Elsa Brenner, "Fighting the John Wayne Syndrome," *New York Times*, November 17, 1991, http://www.nytimes .com/1991/11/17/nyregion/fighting-the-john-wayne -syndrome.html.

7 Robert H. Stein, "Fatherhood of God," in *Baker's Evangelical Dictionary of Biblical Theology*, ed. Walter A. Elwell (Grand Rapids, MI: Baker Books, 1996), http://www .biblestudytools.com/dictionaries/bakers-evangelical -dictionary/fatherhood-of-god.html.

8 H. D. M. Spence, Joseph S. Exell, and Charles Neil, eds., *Thirty Thousand Thoughts, Being Extracts Covering a Comprehensive Circle of Religious and Allied Topics* (New York: Funk & Wagnalls, 1889), https://books.google.com/books ?id=QDsUAAAAYAAJ.

9 Stanley S. Taylor, "Why American Boys Join Street Gangs," *International Journal of Sociology and Anthropology* 5, no. 8 (December 2013): 341.

ABOUT THE AUTHOR

John Finch's mission is to educate, encourage, and equip men to become the fathers they were created to be and to help them walk in daily awareness of their significant and lifelong influence as fathers. He is the founder of The Perfect Father Ministries Inc., the nonprofit organization behind *The Father Effect* documentary; and EncouragingDads.com, a global community sharing short stories to encourage fathers. Along with his wife, Michelle, and their three daughters, John calls Denton, Texas, home.

The Perfect Father Ministries is a 501(c)(3) nonprofit. To donate or learn more, visit TheFatherEffect.com.

Connect with John and The Perfect Father Ministries online at:
https://twitter.com/TheFatherEffect
https://www.facebook.com/The-Father-Effect
-Movie-211007652267276

Made in the USA
Middletown, DE
31 October 2022

13794894R10121